MUSSOLINI ALSO DID A LOT OF GOOD

Francesco Filippi

MUSSOLINI ALSO DID A LOT OF GOOD

The Spread of Historical Amnesia

Translated from the Italian by John Irving

Baraka
Books

Montréal

© Baraka Books

Original title: Mussolini ha fatto anche cose buone. *Le idioze che continuano a circolare sul fascismo* Francesco Filippi, Bollati Boringhieri Editore © 2019

ISBN 978-1-77186-262-2 pbk; 978-1-77186-263-9 epub; 978-1-77186-264-6 pdf

Cover design: Maison 1608
Book Design by Folio infographie
Editing and proofreading: Blossom Thom, Robin Philpot

Legal Deposit, 4th quarter 2021

Bibliothèque et Archives nationales du Québec
Library and Archives Canada

Published by Baraka Books of Montreal

Trade Distribution & Returns
United States – Independent Publishers Group:

IPGbook.com
Canada – UTP Distribution: UTPdistribution.com

Contents

To my wife, Cristina,
who has been waiting for this book
for even longer than I have.

Did Mussolini do any good at all?

Why this book?

"If you tell a big enough lie and keep repeating it, people will eventually come to believe it," is what Joseph Goebbels is alleged to have said when, like a chef proud of one of his recipes, he listed the ingredients for effective totalitarian information. The recipe is still applicable today, all the more so because the media through which a piece of news, be it true or false, moves are infinitely faster than in the Reich Minister of Propaganda's day. In fact, they are so fast that, overwhelmed by the very speed at which more and more new lies are inputted into the system, any attempt at research and refutation is futile. There is no point in debunking *fake news** when people have already moved on to talk about something else: it is to fight a losing battle or, at best, a battle not worth fighting.

---

* In English in the original text.

But if as far as the present is concerned we are forced to wage a gruelling trench war, when dealing with the past it is possible to do a little bit more than that: the advantage of historical fake news is that it is anchored to a specific subject and, once it has been disproved, the truth has the same speed of propagation as the lie it contradicts.

Why is it important to counter this particular type of fake news?

Because history and the recollections that arise from it carry a great weight in the ongoing memory-building of every one of us: if fake news about the present takes root in opinions—which, rightly enough, change according to the stimuli they receive—so fake news about historical facts poisons the immense field of experiences, values and emotions on which we build our image of the past.

Why lie about history?

Speaking about fake news, Marc Bloch, one of the greatest historians of the 20th century and a partisan during the war, explained that, "... it is probably born of imprecise individual observations or imperfect eyewitness accounts, but the original accident is not everything: by itself, it explains nothing. The error propagates itself,

grows, and ultimately survives only on one condition—that it finds a favorable cultural broth
in the society where it is spreading. Through it,
people unconsciously express all their prejudices,
hatreds, fears, all their strong emotions. Only
great collective states of mind [...] have the power
to transform a misperception into a legend."[1]

Hence, while fake news about the present
serves to orient the public opinion at which it is
targeted, fake news about history has the deeper
purpose of buoying up the feelings and emotions
of those who are prepared to accept it. A lie about
the past is reassuring and confirms feelings about
which we would otherwise feel ashamed, setting
comforting benchmarks, be they true or false.

Demolishing a piece of historical fake news
thus has two effects: first, it corrects the body of
information about the past that we use to build
our own individual memories and the single collective memory, a use we might define as "neutral"
or, at the most, "reparatory." The second effect,
which is harder to deal with, is the destruction
of certainties and presumed facts in the listener,
a dangerous phenomenon that risks erecting a
wall of incommunicability. A certainty cannot be
demolished with impunity. This, unfortunately,
is why the job of demolishing historical falsities
serves no purpose in amending the behavior of
the spreaders of this kind of news. Yet it is a job
that needs to be done if we are to circumscribe

the range of dissemination of fake news that poisons memory and, as a result, perception of the present. Debunking a lie that is going the rounds on the internet will not change the minds of nonsense mongers, but it does help web surfers to recognise and stave off sources of fake news.

Just as knowing about the past is a way of understanding its mechanisms and gaining awareness of the present, so being familiar with and denying lies about it are a way of uncovering the dangers of poor memory and preventing the damage it can cause.

It seems significant in this regard that one of the figures about whom most lies are told in Italy is Benito Mussolini, a man who dominated twenty years of European history, now remote enough in time to be dismissed as nothing other than a piece of history, but about whom legends and untruths, largely positive, continue to flourish. Much of the fake news about Fascism was born of Fascism itself, and some of it caught on at moments in which desperate attempts were being made to set a benign past against a negative present. As is the case today.

Umberto Eco used to say that, "Mussolini did not have a philosophy, he had only rhetoric."[2] It is thus normal, especially today, for Fascism to assume the characteristics not so much of an historical ideology as of a public narrative, not a succession of ideas but a mythical tale of lost happiness. Spreading positive snippets of memory about a man who, as we shall see, was, de facto, the greatest butcher of Italians in history is of no use to historiography, and experts in the sector can smell fake news about the *Duce* from a long way off. But it is useful, very useful indeed, to create emotions, as in a pleasant story, a fable told to reassure, or to issue a warning.

Thinking back to a hypothetical positive past puts hope in the heart of anyone who is unhappy with their present. At a time when everything moves so fast and values are fluid, having a safe, quiet place to find shelter is reassuring, even if that place is memory and that memory is false. In Mussolini's case, making up lies about the past also serves to concoct a simple and effective account of the present, a prospect worth striving for. The famous saying "When He was around!" is at once a reassurance about the past and a veiled threat about the present, which translates into "If only *He* were to come back," or even more explicitly, "*When He* or someone like *Him* comes back."

The basis for a possible totalitarian future depends partly on the rehabilitation of the totalitarian past. Evincing the reality of that past is the first step to prevent it from becoming the future.

CHAPTER 1

Mussolini the Provident and Prudential

Was the *Duce* the first man to give Italians pensions?

Pensions are one of the pet subjects of those who look back with nostalgia to the Fascist period, publicly and virtually. The idea, still comparatively widespread, is that having taken power, it was Mussolini who built the Italian welfare system and gave everyone the chance to enjoy their old age serenely through a modern system of social security contributions. In addition to the pension system, the Fascist state is also said to have activated the principal forms of social welfare and regulation of working conditions. This complex system, worthy of a regime attentive to the needs of its citizens, allegedly gave Italians workplace security and the right to decent old-age pensions.

"He provided all Italians with free welfare!"

Pensions—or, better still, the welfare system for old-age and sickness benefits—were actually a German invention, which made their first appearance thanks to Chancellor Otto von Bismarck. The law on old age and invalidity insurance was introduced in the German Empire in 1888:[1] it was a system that, on payment of contributions, entrusted the state with taking economic care of those workers who, for reasons of old age or infirmity, had become unfit for work. This veritable social revolution subsequently spread across the rest of industrialized Europe.

Birth of the pension system in Italy (1895-1919)

It was the Francesco Crispi* government that officially adopted a guaranteed pension system for the first time in Italy in 1895, twenty-seven years before the Fascists took power. Royal Decree no. 70 of February 21, 1895,[2] entitled public sector white-collar workers and servicemen to a

---

* Francesco Crispi (1818–1901), Sicilian politician and leading player in the Risorgimento. Famous for his anticlerical views, he was twice prime minister, from 1887 to 1891 and from 1893 until 1896. (translator's note)

form of social security protection in the event of their reaching retirement age or suffering from crippling diseases. Implementational regulations also provided for the activation of survivor pensions for widows and orphans. Three years later, the Pelloux government adopted Law no. 350 of 1898[3] guaranteeing insurance coverage for a number of professional categories. At the same time, the National Workers' Invalidity and Retirement Fund (Cassa nazionale di Previdenza per l'invalidità e la vecchiaia degli operai) was set up to manage contributions and provide welfare services for workers.

At first, the system was voluntary, supported by the state with incentives to the companies that adhered to it. Thanks, above all, to the struggles of the Italian trade unions, it soon spread to the country's most important blue-collar categories.

When World War I broke out, a series of welfare provisions was thus provided for civil servants, soldiers and factory workers. The labour unrest and the risk of a drift to revolution provoked by the conflict obliged the government to promise further reforms in order to maintain social peace and sustain the war effort. With the war over, a new set of social reforms introduced further protections in 1919.[4]

The pension sector was reformed radically: the old Invalidity and Retirement Fund became the National Social Insurance Fund (Cassa Nazionale per le Assicurazioni Sociali), adherence to the system was made compulsory for employers, and trade union representatives were allowed to sit on the body's board of directors. The change in the Fund's name suggested that guaranteed protection was no longer to be a benefit for the individual worker but was to be extended to society as a whole. From that moment on—from 1919, that is—all Italian workers were entitled to a pension by law.

The nucleus of social security in Italy, put in place within the framework of reforms implemented by Francesco Crispi's Historical Left,* was subsequently developed as a system of universal security by Vittorio Emanuele Orlando's Liberal government.

Fascist measures (1922-1939)

After conquering power, Mussolini at once undertook to take control of this vital sector of the state apparatus. The first change to the system as a whole—the abolition of Ministry of Labor and Welfare—ordered by the Royal Decree of April 27, 1923[5]—was at once symbolic and substantial. It was a way of making clear that labor

---

* The Historical Left was a political reform movement in power between 1876 and 1896, later described as 'Historical' to distinguish it from twentieth-century left-wing movements. (translator's note)

and welfare did not have a political autonomy of their own, but were merely one part of the centralizing body into which the government was being transformed. The functions, hence the command levers, of ministries such as the Treasury, firmly in the hands of Mussolini's staunchest followers, were all centralized. On May 4, 1923, the top management of the National Social Insurance Fund was ousted and replaced by Mussolini's henchmen and representatives of philo-Fascist labour unions.[6]

At that time, the Fund was still essentially a financial institution. Its main duties were the collection of insured workers' premiums and the distribution of pension benefits. When he took control, Mussolini began to supplement the Fund's original services, such as invalidity and old age coverage for specific professional categories and social protection, with many of the ones previously provided by professional social security and welfare structures. In 1924, for example, the job of managing involuntary unemployment insurance was assigned to the Fund,[7] followed in 1927 by paramedical services such as the management of tuberculosis insurance.[8]

The precise purpose of taking over management duties was to centralize in a single body, directly controllable by the executive, the many forms of social care and security that had sprung up over the years alongside public welfare structures. The clear aim was to control any form of social assistance, de facto placing benefits under the aegis of the state, meaning the Fascist Party. The Fund was changing its original function by concentrating all the public interventions that we would now refer to as welfare. Fascism thus merely limited itself to amalgamating what existed in Italy already.

These maneuvers were not accompanied by a concomitant expansion of the structures of the Fund, which struggled initially to cope with its new duties. Albeit now "domesticated," the board of directors signalled this lack of balance on more than one occasion, and even complained to the government about it.[9] Paradoxically, Fascism's first social security provisions weighed down the system and made it progressively inefficient. Instead of improving it, the reforms had the sole aim of subduing it and enabling the highest authorities to control it directly.

"Mussolini gave us pensions!"

Appropriation of social security structures reached its climax in 1933 when the Fascist regime decided to make a blanket reform of the Fund as a whole. The most visible—and significant—effect of the reform was another change: the Cassa Nazionale, or National Fund, became the Fascist

National Insurance Institute (Istituto Nazionale Fascista della Previdenza Sociale), whose unpronounceable acronym was INFPS.[10] Adding the term "Fascist" was a propagandistic attempt to take over what was actually the fruit of decades of trade union bargaining and struggles, of reforms enacted by Liberal governments, and of the initiatives of professional labor associations.

In addition to the change in name, amendments were made to the social security machine's setup. The structure of the Institute, which had grown into one of the largest government bodies of the time, was verticalized by concentrating in the president's hands prerogatives and responsibilities that had previously been spread over organs of administration such as the board of directors. As is easily imaginable, the appointment of this new "super-president" was made directly by the head of government, Benito Mussolini himself.

The Fascists did not invent social security in Italy with this crucial reform, they simply took it over. Once they had occupied this portion of the public sector permanently, the regime turned INFPS into a great payer of wages: in 1941, the number of direct employees reached 8,000, making the Institute the second largest public employer in Italy.[11] Working for INFPS became a dream for a large section of lower middle-class white-collar workers, the hard core of the Fascist consensus. In 1939, the tragi-comic episode of INFPS president Bruno Biagi's having to publish an appeal in all the major Italian dailies begging job hunters to stop sending in applications, "because the Institute does not need personnel," showed just how high people's expectations were in this regard.[12]

In the course of time, employees in secure well-paid jobs were joined by a mass of professionals, temporary employees and workers. On paper, they were supposed to act as a stopgap in performing the body's many extraordinary functions but, in reality, became a stable source of consensus for the regime. When membership of the Fascist Party was made compulsory to hold public office, a great many people rushed to apply for jobs—if need be, temporary—as social security personnel.

To regulate this onslaught by loyal Fascists, real or professed, a special law even had to be passed: Law no. 782 of May 29, 1939, in fact, eloquently entitled "Temporary employment of members of Fascist action squads* in state administration offices and other public bodies."[13] With this legislation, public administrations were obliged to employ anyone able to document

---

* *Squadristi* from *squadre d'azione*, Fascist militias organized outside the authority of the Italian state. (translator's note)

long-term Fascist Party membership. Certificates of merit and lengthy militancy could obviously only be bestowed by the best-known members of the Party and the pursuit of Fascist action squad membership cards became a way like any other of fuelling the patronage systems of local and national bosses, known as *ras*.*

At the same time, the Institute became a veritable night safe from which the regime plundered extraordinary funds and contributions for the most diverse purposes, including land reclamation consortia, extraordinary provisions and state-controlled welfare agencies close to the regime. These were just a few of the thousand streams into which trickled money collected from workers' contributions and which was spent for purposes other than institutional ones. When the Fascist regime entered the war, it marked the coup de grâce for the coffers of the Institute. It found itself having to process the claims for compensation from invalids and widows of soldiers at the front, while its offices became a safe haven for those seeking to shirk military service and the draft.

---

* Traditional aristocratic title in Ethiopia. Following the Italian invasion of the country the term was adopted in colloquial Italian to refer to local Fascist powerbrokers. (translator's note)

After Fascism

With the fall of the regime, the adjective "Fascist"[14] was removed from the name of the Institute to form the acronym, INPS, which still operates today. After the war, its functions were reviewed and, in part, rationalized. The broadening of the social security base to create the arrangement we are familiar with today was only finalized in 1969, thanks to the efforts of Socialist Giacomo Brodolini.

Brodolini was the one who drove through republican Italy's most important national insurance reform, Law no. 153 of 1969,[15] which, among other things, provided for the institution of the so-called *"pensione sociale,"* or social pension. This meant economic support for everyone aged 65 and over, whether they had paid in their contributions or not.

In addition to the "banner" pension story, nostalgic revisionism around the *Duce* feeds off other myths. Yet even for the other worker protection provisions for which the regime is given credit, it appears to have very few merits.

What about the tredicesima?

The Fascist regime did issue some social policy decrees for given categories. One attempt to broaden the base of workers' rights has since given grounds for a piece of blatantly fake news that we often find bruited in the social media. Typical of the festive period, it refers to the *tredicesima*, or "thirteenth month," the year-end employees' bonus. Many people still argue that it was thanks to the *Duce* that the provision has ended up rewarding millions of Italians every year. But if we analyze the Fascist legislation, we discover that the claim is not simply an exaggeration, it is downright wrong.

The phenomenon of the employee's wage packet bonus was a widespread, if unregulated, practice in many European countries, especially in France and Germany. As far as the Italian system is concerned, for virtually the duration of the Fascist period this type of bonus was paid at the employer's discretion. The thirteenth monthly wage, known as the "Christmas bonus," was officially introduced to article 13 of the national collective labour agreement for factory workers by the Chamber of Fasces and Corporations on August 5, 1937.[16] No other category was added to those deserving of end-of-year bonus pay. The legislation did not extend the rights of workers as a whole, but was an ad hoc provision for a category that was a vast source of political support for the regime: namely the so-called white-collar workers who formed the Italian lower middle class and dreamt of a secure job to free them from precariousness. These were the people likely to sing "*Se potessi avere mille lire al mese*" (If only I could have a thousand lire a month).[17]

The 1937 collective agreement did offer this sectional benefit, but it also tightened up legislation on overtime work for the same category. As article 8 of the agreement states, "For personnel with discontinuous duties, the working hours will normally envisage a maximum of ten hours a day; the number of hours may be increased to twelve a day for certain duties, if expressly determined in supplementary agreements. Within the limits allowed by the law, no clerical worker may refuse to perform overtime, night and holiday work, barring justified reasons of impediment."[18] Working hours were thus imposed to bind workers' rights to the necessities of industry, de facto limiting their freedom.

As to the thirteenth month bonus, the majority of factory workers, both unskilled and skilled, had to wait until the end of the war to receive it. It was, in fact, the inter-confederation agreement of October 27, 1946, the first in the industrial sector in the history of the Italian Republic, that extended the extra monthly benefit to all factory workers without distinction. But it was only with the decree of the President of the Republic no. 1070 of 1960, at the height of Italy's economic miracle, that the protocol for factory workers' pay was extended to all workers, becoming a worker's right and not just a concession achieved through union agreements.[19]

... and the Cassa Integrazione?

The provision for the Cassa Integrazione Guadagni (CIG) redundancy fund—the system that props up the wages of workers at firms in distress—is sometimes attributed to the *Duce*'s desire to support business. Scanning labor legislation, however, it would appear that the first forms of wage integration and support for workers at floundering firms were introduced to the system only after the foundation of the republic. To all intents and purposes, the CIG was only activated by the decree of the Provisional Head of State no. 869 of 1947.[20]

The provisions that really affected workers' lives

In addition to what the Fascists are erroneously said to have done, it might also be useful to recall what they actually did do in the field of workers' rights. Law no. 563 of April 3, 1926, has gone down in history as one of the so-called "*leggi fascistissime,*" a set of "very Fascist" laws that changed the nature of the Italian state to make it positively totalitarian. It was entitled "Rules and regulations governing collective labor relations"[21] and it established that only categories of workers in associations officially recognized by the state would be eligible for union representation. Even then, however, the only associations to be officially recognized were the Fascist ones. This was a way of ensuring the regime's full control over every aspect of working people's lives.

Article 18 of the same law forbade strikes and lockouts, and threatened anyone attempting to strike with fines and imprisonment. It should be noted that whereas the prohibition of strikes was an attack on the freedom of action of union representatives, prohibiting lockouts—the arbitrary closure of factories—meant that employers and their activities were placed under close control too. This was the first step towards what Fascist economic theory was to dub the "corporative state,"[22] whereby national production had to be placed under the control of the state and bent to its needs.

To consolidate this takeover and make conciliation in worker-employer relations one of the pillars of consensus, a special Ministry of Corporations was set up in the same year.[23] This action of centralization and appropriation of the control of employer-employee relations continued with the establishment of the Chamber of Fasces and Corporations,[24] an institution that replaced the Chamber of Deputies. Its functions, which were theoretically legislative in character, were supposed to represent Italian productive society as a whole, but insofar as it was composed of members of all the main Fascist organizations, it became nothing more than a battleground for the Party's various rival factions.[25]

The regime's activity in the fields of social security and in labor issues in general always had a clear political intent, especially in the later stages of the dictatorship. When consensus for the regime was beginning to fray, Mussolini used interventions in welfare for propaganda purposes. In an attempt to maintain consensus at pre-war levels, "the regime reiterated the populist issues"[26] that had created the basis for its initial program.

In conclusion, Fascist legislative measures in social security moved in two main directions. First, they sought to consolidate the Party's hold over given social sectors by amending the social welfare and security structure to make it easy to control, and by limiting workers' rights. Secondly, they aimed to turn the state's massive administrative apparatus into a machine at the service of Fascism by transforming it into a distributor of public money and a provider of jobs for hangers-on. The machine was more a builder of consensus than of well-being and security for Italians.

CHAPTER 2

Mussolini the Champion of Land Reclamation

Did the *Duce* drain the marshes?

Over the years, the Fascists' apparent success in the area of *bonifica* or land reclamation has become the epitome of the "good" the *Duce* did for his people. Today, even as other presumed successes are being questioned, the reclamation of marshland is still a cornerstone of the narrative of the regime's effectiveness and efficiency. But if we contextualize the issue and analyze the results achieved during the twenty years of Fascist rule, this myth too risks exploding.

The situation before 1922

Historically, some parts of Italy, such as the Po Delta and the so-called Pontine marshes in the Lazio region, were characterized by the presence of wetlands. These were insalubrious, inhospitable areas unsuited for farming and, in the olden days, the haunt of outlaws. Malaria, a veritable endemic scourge, had been rife there since antiquity. The spread of the disease was so vast in the country's regions that it became the "Italian disease" par excellence, hence the use of the Italian word for it in many European languages. Insecurity, danger and disease made the marshes risky, obscure, baleful places. In Italy, the struggle against these inhospitable districts had gone on for centuries, the first documentation of attempts to regiment water and reclaim marshland dating back to the Roman era.

Systematic reclamation work was launched by the papacy in the fifteenth century but achieved only limited results, while the Kingdom of Italy also embarked on schemes to sanitize the swampy areas near Rome and in the north of the country.[1] The first organic law for the reclamation of the marshes was passed in 1878,[2] after which the decree that underpinned all special legislation for the malarial regions in the course of the twentieth century was only issued in 1905.[3] The question of the reclamation of these districts for human settlement became one of the yardsticks for judging the efficiency (or inefficiency) of the Italian political class.

But did Mussolini really win this epochal challenge? It has to be said that the marshes were an outstanding propaganda showcase issue right from the outset. For the regime's narrative it was a perfect cause to exploit: following in the footsteps of the ancient Romans, the Fascists allegedly brought malarial land back to life and made it fertile, productive and welcoming: there could be no comparison with the ineptitude of previous governments.

In reality, however, browsing through the legislation of the period, we can see how, at least from the normative point of view, public efforts were already being concentrated on the problem before Mussolini took power. In 1922 alone, even before the March on Rome, as many as twenty royal decrees were issued to expand the scope of state interventions on marshlands with the setting up of state-subsidized reclamation consortia. Wartime conditions had led to a fresh upsurge of cases of malaria and the loss of whole areas of reclaimed land in Veneto and Friuli, and in the post-First World War years, the problem of the marshes assumed the proportions of a veritable national health emergency. According to the surveys of the commission set up to coordinate reclamation operations, in the 1920s, eight million hectares of land were drainable, with consequent benefits for the health of citizens.

"But you can't deny that it was he who reclaimed the marshes!"

Fascist measures

Once at the helm, the Fascists picked up the gaunt-
let by passing a series of laws and implementing
precise policies, and on December 30, 1923, a consolidation act on land reclamation[4] rationalized
and combined all previous legislative measures
into a single provision. In this as in other cases,
Mussolini did not invent new ways of addressing
the problem but succeeded in the feat of reunify-
ing the many initiatives already underway and of
taking the credit for their implementation.

The consolidation act provided for subdivision
of land into areas of primary and secondary reclamation, applying to the first an emergency legal
regime favoring direct state intervention and the
concession of loans and subsidies. This approach
failed to produce any notable effects at first.
Indeed, especially in the south of Italy, there were
vocal protests from *latifondisti* who happened
to own malarial land: the expropriation system,
though it provided generous compensation, jeop-
ardised their control over their estates and risked
filling local areas with small independent landowners. The big landowners' opposition to the
first Fascist schemes caused the most ambitious
measures to be suspended and brought about
the resignation from the government of Arrigo
Serpieri, the economist who had drawn up the
eminent domain legislation.

It is clear therefore that in what Fascist propaganda had pompously dubbed the "water war,"[5] the line of rigid state intervention personified by Serpieri, had lost its first battle. The Fascists collided with centuries-old resistance to land reclamation and appeared from the start to be enjoying no greater fortune than the Liberal governments that had preceded it.

The principle of the consolidated act of December 30, 1923, was that alongside direct state intervention, with the setting up and subsidizing of public land reclamation consortia, a large share of work should be carried out by private interests. The idea was that if the state managed to make reclamation schemes economically advantageous for the private sector, the sector itself would shoulder most of the work involved in conquering land and maintaining finished projects. For this reason, a large chunk of private investment was allocated to subsidizing loans, unsecured grants and transfers of state public land to anyone prepared to carry out reclamation work. Unfortunately for the regime, the Italian farming sector, which had been seriously weakened by the war and the peasant unrest of the early 1920s and a consequent reduction of the workforce, failed to recover. In fact, it slumped increasingly as decidedly more competitive agricultural goods arrived on the market from overseas. Not only were there no resources and men available to conquer new productive lands, the productivity of land already put to crop was also falling. The private sector would not support Fascism in its propaganda campaign.

Despite the pledges made to public opinion, drainage and reclamation were failing to produce the results hoped for. So in 1926, the regime attempted to give the project a boost by adopting a provision that tasked the Opera Nazionale Combattenti (ONC), or National Veterans Association, with actively improving farming in economically depressed areas.[6] This proved to be a good move on Mussolini's part: the ONC was a very powerful association that provided assistance to World War I veterans and their families. It amounted, in practice, to an enormous employment office for ex-servicemen still in search of employment, who represented a vast source of consensus in favor of Fascism that required continuous largess. Entrusting them with the task of reclamation meant ensuring veterans with socially useful work and, at once, finding new hands for the water war.

To avoid any misunderstanding as to the ONC's new duties, article 2 of the relevant decree made clear that, "The Opera may have the government grant provided for by royal decree no. 3139 of December 30, 1923, paid to it directly on the basis of the amount of the sums borrowed for works of land and agrarian improvement."[7]

The provision was a mandate to engage in reclamation work and maintain the promises of Fascism with all the economic advantages this entailed. The Fascists' initial idea of propping up the reclamation system through temporary public intervention with limited financial outlay had floundered. It thus moved from an approach based on state-private sector collaboration to one of resolute state intervention. This consisted largely of subsidies to the ONC, now an elephantine structure with considerable political and public clout. It was a leap from liberalism to the unalloyed welfarism among friendly agencies.

However, not even the deployment of legions of ex-servicemen managed to shake up the situation. The amount of land clawed back from water was still marginal compared to the enormity of the challenge undertaken by the regime. This is why, five years on from the first provisions, the decision was taken to take remedial action with a new set of laws.

On Christmas Eve 1928, the government passed the law on integral reclamation,[8] to which the *Duce* gave his name to express just how much he was staking his own image on the measure. It was thus that the Mussolini Law on reclamation relaunched the question of the elimination of the scourge of malaria in propagandistic terms. An ad hoc undersecretaryship was established within the Ministry of Agriculture and the *Duce* described the marshland campaign as "an effort that will make a people proud and create an everlasting claim to glory for the Fascist regime."[9]

But the law failed to introduce any real innovations, consisting essentially of a long list of long-term spending commitments with promises that were to prove onerous for the public finances. Its budget allocations for 1930-31, the first fiscal year to which it was to apply, earmarked 13.5 million lire for irrigation and reclamation schemes. Allocations were subsequently to increase year by year to reach the staggering figure of 257 million lire in the 1943-44 budget. The Mussolini Law stated that it would keep annual funds available for reclamation work at least until 1959-60.[10]

The Law was an attempt to ensure prolonged state support to anyone reclaiming land and promised rivers of money to anyone who had collaborated in the scheme. It is interesting, however, to note the disproportion between the funds made available by the measure immediately and those promised for the future. The difference betrays the propagandistic nature of the law: if the intention had been the one declared—namely to kickstart the reclamation scheme—it would have been logical to earmark a large allocation immediately to shake the works that had been promised in 1923 out of the stagnation in which they were bogged down ("bog" being the operative word). Instead, partly on account of budget

difficulties and the agricultural crisis, the legis-
lator preferred to reserve the sums necessary for
future budgets much later in time.

Instead of scaling down objectives to take
account of the difficulties involved in implementing the work promised, government propaganda upped the ante with high-sounding figures. In addition to the quarter of a billion lire
promised for every fiscal year henceforth, the
regime declared its intention to reclaim and
convert for farming the eight million hectares
of land still regarded as insalubrious. This was
a huge amount if we consider that, at the time,
in the whole of Italy just over 27 million hectares of land—five and a half a million of which
were woodland—were given over to farming.[11] In
practice, the Fascists promised to increase the
country's workable farming land by one third.

In a situation that was hardly realistic at the
time, the 1929 world economic crash made the
budget commitments totally *unrealistic* and
pushed the estimates for the prospective reclamation work off the scale. Due to lack of funding
at many sites, be they promised or already under
way, very few projects were actually completed.
As the economic historian Rolf Petri writes,
"Many reclamation consortia announced the
commencement of work, but often only formal-
ly."[12] Projects were thus started without a guaranteed budget in the hope that the government

might raise the money necessary at some stage in the future.

The money flow that the regime channelled into the so-called "Battle for Land" ended up largely in major hydraulics projects, managed as we have seen by ONC, or the National Veterans Association. For years, reclamation work was carried out with public investment, which on the one hand constituted a sizable expenditure item and on the other was insufficient to cover the cost of the projects announced. At this point, however, the magnitude of the commitment undertaken and its consequences for the public image of Fascism were such that there was no going back.

If reclamation could not be carried out properly, at least it had to be narrated well. This is why the second phase of the "water war," announced by the 1928 law, was characterized by a veritable instrumentalization of the pledge to conquer land. Land that had to be made not only productive but also hospitable.

Besides draining the malarial plains and making them fertile, efforts were also made to render them habitable in order to be able to count on a permanent garrison in the "Battle for Land." This too was a major advertising campaign in which the myth of the reconquest of land was, very effectively, likened to ancient Roman colonization: as had happened two thousand years earlier, gallant Italic colonists would challenge adversity to win new land for civilization.[13] Whole new towns were built from scratch to house colonists deported from the rest of Italy to make the symbol of new Italian agriculture grow.

In a nation in which, for a great many, the only means of survival was emigration, demonstrating that new land to work had been created was viewed as a great achievement. Peasants from the lowest levels of agricultural society were moved to the new districts. Most of the colonists in the *Agro pontino*, the Pontine marshes, came from the Veneto, Emilia and Friuli regions. At first, the *Duce* was skeptical about the decision to urbanize the reclaimed land, but soon changed his mind when he understood the symbolic value of new towns being founded under the aegis of Fascism. Just like the ancient Romans two thousand years earlier, Mussolini was able to say that he had founded new towns and cities. The largest of these, inaugurated on December 18, 1932, obviously by the dictator himself, was christened in honour of Fascist power as Littoria,* after the party symbol.

It was precisely in this period that the great Fascist myth of the deliverance of the land was

---

* Situated just south of Rome, Littoria was founded in 1931. It was named for the lictors, the law enforcers of ancient Rome whose weapon, the *fasces*, rods tied with rope and topped by a sharpened axe, adopted by the National Fascist Party as its symbol. The town was renamed Latina in 1945. (translator's note) born. The comparison between the ability to make ancient Italian land physically healthy and inhabitable and that of making the government of the country also clean, decent and active again by cleansing political life and colonizing it with new forces was very effective indeed. The myth of the reclamation of the swamps was so well constructed that it is the most resilient and least questioned of all the fake news that circulates about Fascism.

Exactly ten years after the introduction of the measures that gave life to the "water war," the Fascist regime, with impressive symbols like the new Pontine towns under its belt, declared victory. It did so with a new law, which was to provide the normative framework for the management of the new lands and the reclamation consortia, and also set out the obligations of the owners of the new plots. Law 215 of 1933[14] sanctioned a new phase in the land reclamation process, seeking on the one hand to normalize management in the wake of the initial pioneering phase, on the other correcting evident errors in the development model for the new land.

Most of the law's 121 articles were devoted to establishing the landowners' obligations. These included maintenance of canals, indispensable for salubriousness, and a ban against accumulating too many reclaimed plots that could be sublet for profit. Some of the articles, however, prolonged the benefits envisaged for colonists, such as a five-year exemption from the payment of land taxes. Others were introduced to further regulate the duties, obligations and, above all, fiscal and financial benefits of local land reclamation consortia. This series of articles paints a picture that shows clearly that the 1923 and 1928 legislation was often ignored. It is also possible to deduct that the existence of the colonists was anything but easy if, in addition to guaranteeing benefits, it was also deemed necessary to take measures to discourage people from abandoning the land.

The first management system envisaged by the Fascists, that of public support for private initiative contained in the 1923 guidelines, had failed. The second system, adopted in 1928 with heftier state intervention and co-opted into the ONC operation, would appear to demonstrate what had already been clear in the mid-1920s: namely that though the burden of primary reclamation weighed on the pockets of taxpayers, cultivating the land clawed back from the water was not economically attractive for private individuals. The solution proposed by the 1933 law—obliging colonists to cling on to their land and prolong easy-term loans and tax relief in the hope that the situation might one day improve—was thus the only way to avoid losing face.

"He thought about reclaiming land, today's politicians about claiming money."

Difficulties of a practical nature aside, what was the real impact of land reclamation on the expectations created by the regime? A glance at the data takes much of the edge off the triumphalist tones of the time. The Fascists had squared up to the challenge of recovering eight million hectares of new land for civilization. After ten years of work and spending public money, the government declared it had achieved the target it had set itself, proclaiming that four million hectares of land were ready for the plow. That was only half the land declared as the target at the start of the Battle for Land but, given the size of the area involved, it was nonetheless a notable result.

The problem is that if we study the figures carefully, it becomes obvious that only a little more than two million hectares of the four mentioned were actually ready, or almost ready. And of these two million, one and a half had been reclaimed by pre-1922 governments.[15] So given that of the four million hectares touted, two million were only works in progress, or imagined, and another million and a half were the fruit of pre-Fascist reclamation work, it is possible to conclude that target of eight million hectares of land scheduled for reclamation was missed by seven and a half million. In practice, only a little more than 6 percent of the work planned had actually been completed.

Speaking about the government's commitment to land reclamation, Renzo De Felice, one of Italy's leading historians of Fascism, made clear that, "Overall, the results of integral reclamation were inferior not only to those scheduled in his original plan by Serpieri (who, not coincidentally, after trying in vain to relaunch it, left the under-secretaryship for integral reclamation in January 1935), but also to the expectations raised in the country by the massive propaganda campaign, and were eventually disproportionate to the magnitude of the economic effort sustained."[16]

The greatest failure of the reclamation program was the regime's inability to involve private individuals in the management of its ordinary maintenance. The delicate water flow system required regular daily care and cleaning, a commitment that colonists could only meet by devoting to it much of the work they should have been doing in the fields. The Fascist-designed reclamation system was neither economically nor socially sustainable. The premises underpinning the regime's solution were wrong and the correctives ineffective, so the work remained largely incomplete. The problem of marshlands was not solved by Mussolini.

Malaria

Though the regime treated reclamation as a strictly agrarian question and placed the emphasis on its agricultural functions, another broad front was still open in the marshlands: that of the fight against malaria.

But understanding exactly how effective this particular fight was is more complex. Studying the annuals in the archives of the Italian National Institute of Statistics (ISTAT), it is possible to reconstruct the spread of malaria in Italy quite accurately from the early years of the twentieth century.[17] Malaria was one of the infectious diseases the reporting of which to the public health authorities was compulsory.

The data vary greatly: in the first survey available, from 1902, 177,946 cases were recorded, while in the period between 1902 and the advent of Fascism, figures fluctuated from a maximum of 323,312 cases in 1905 to a minimum of 129,482 in 1914. The Great War brought a fresh outbreak of the disease and in 1922, on the eve of the Fascist declaration of the Battle for Land, reported sufferers numbered 234,656. The figure fell to 180,000 in 1923, but rose again the next year to more than 250,000. The progress of the disease was obviously subject to variation for the most diverse factors, but in the first ten years under Fascist rule, the number of cases only dropped below 200,000 in 1927 (192,738). By 1933 the number had fallen to 175,000 but ballooned again the following year to 222,171. It was only after 1935 that cases began to drop steadily, and in 1939 only 55,000 suffered from malaria.

Part of the credit for the decline must certainly be attributed to the decrease in the number of malarial regions. From analysis of the data, however, it would appear that if the evolution of reclamation schemes had been that officially declared by the regime, mortality rate did not follow the curve that might have been expected. If, in 1922, there had been 4,000 deaths, in 1927 the number had dropped to 2,500, before exceeding 3,000 again in 1931 and 1932. Such discordance may be explained by considering not only the number of hectares of land reclaimed (or declared as being reclaimed) but also the preventive anti-malarial treatment given to the population.

In Italy, the monopoly sector oversaw, among other things, the public distribution of quinine, the medicine used at the time to combat the disease. The data on state subsidies to the public distribution of quinine in historical data sets[18] show that the sums allocated by the Fascist government to preventive treatment were always high, around 15 million lire a year, and increased in the 1930s at the same pace as the fall in the disease. Malaria thus retreated into endemic areas more thanks to preventive treatment than to reclamation work. Indeed, it is possible that the peak in infectiousness and mortality of 1931 and 1932 was directly attributable to the fact that, due to the massive excavation work needed to construct waterways, many more people were exposed to infection without adequate preventive treatment.

When, during the war of liberation, the battlefront swept over the reclaimed areas and brought maintenance work to a halt, the Germans only had to block a few canal discharges to provoke an environmental catastrophe that wiped out the work of decades and returned malaria to endemic levels. In 1944, 144,000 cases were recorded.

Only in the post-war years did other massive reclamation schemes—funded by the US Marshall Plan and the Cassa del Mezzogiorno, the Fund for the South—drain Italian marshland extensively and stably. Credit for the easing of malaria was due not only to preventive treatment but also to mass-spraying with the DDT imported by the Americans. After the war, it took another twenty-five years of international efforts to maintain the promise contained in Mussolini's 1923 declarations and the World Health Organization declared that malaria had been finally eradicated in Italy only in 1970.[19]

CHAPTER 3

Mussolini the Builder

Did the *Duce* give all Italians a home to live in?

Italians are a people of homeowners.[1] The home is the main expense in the lives of many Italians, who consider it fundamental for the realization of their life projects. Even article 47 of the Republican Constitution asserts that one of the state's fundamental duties is to help its citizens— economically, if necessary—to own their own homes.[2]

This is why associating the right to a home with Fascism is one of the most effective, impactful posthumous propagandist operations for the rehabilitation of the dictatorship. Whereas matters such as the regime's relationship with the rule of law and human rights may be a source of criticism or relativization, allowing the *Duce* credit for "giving Italians a home" is an image-enhancing and efficient expedient. It is, however, based on unrealistic premises.

The housing problem in Liberal Italy

From the second half of the nineteenth century, the Italian peninsula experienced an unprecedented population boom: the Kingdom of Italy, between its birth and its end in 1946, saw its population increase from just over 22 million to 46 million.[3] This social revolution had a huge impact on town planning: notwithstanding mass emigration, all the large Italian towns and cities recorded a dizzy increase in the number of their inhabitants. Their urban fabric, often still medieval in structure, was incapable of sustaining the growth. The problem of housing was thus at the center of the post-Unity public debate and meeting the demand for houses became essentially the responsibility of local administrations.

The central government's first intervention to support the right to housing for all citizens came in 1903 with a law on housing projects.[4] This measure, which was passed largely as a result of the work of Luigi Luzzatti, a member of parliament on the historical right, laid the bases for state involvement: it was the first piece of legislation to provide for "legally formed cooperative societies with the sole purpose of building, purchasing and selling or leasing social housing to members."[5] It also set the criteria for the concessional funding of this type of association, which soon became the centre of the Italian housing

evolution. In 1906, the granting of the qualification "moral entities" to the first social housing
institutes[6]—which also envisaged, among other
things, special taxation parameters—sanctioned
their public utility and established housing as a
problem subject to direct public intervention.

Attempts had already been made to address
the housing problem at the local level prior to
Law 254 in 1903. The 1903 law was another stage
in a process of institutionalization of worthy
experiences as a stimulus to foster new ones.
Luzzatti had the insight to supplement delocal-
ized systems for managing the problem with
unifying, but not centralizing, legislation at
national level. His was a diffuse system of local
cooperatives that catered to the needs of individual communes by accessing preferential credit
channels according to a non-speculative conception of social housing.[7] It is thus fair to say
that if anyone deserves to be remembered as the
"father of social housing" in Italy, it is the Liberal
Luigi Luzzatti.

The new institutes appeared where the housing problem was most serious: in Rome, a city
that had witnessed a population boom following the unification of Italy. Whole neighborhoods, such as Garbatella, sprang up in the first
decades of the twentieth century. Most of the
major urban development projects in Italy's
largest cities were launched before the advent

of Fascism: in 1907, the Istituto case popolari (Popular Housing Institute) was established in Turin,[8] and in Naples[9] and Milan the following year.[10] The same year saw the publication of general social housing regulations,[11] with guidelines for the management of the legal and economic aspects of the building of new homes.

Fascist measures

Insofar as the phenomenon of social housing had been set in motion and regulated long before the advent of Fascism, Fascist housing policies did not have to be innovative. Their aim was to stimulate the initiatives of individual communes by promoting expansion projects in the various towns and cities and, above all, supporting the institutes that already existed. Housing policy, however, remained an essentially local initiative.

Something changed with the 1935 law decentralizing the social housing management system and forming a national consortium.[12] De facto, the new law changed the name of local autonomous bodies that had existed for decades, while centralizing their control structure. The social housing institutes in large communes came under provincial jurisdiction and their presidents were appointed by royal decree, while their names were proposed by the Ministry of Labor. At the same time, the foundation of the national consortium of the new institutes, which was obviously a direct expression of the regime, completed the Fascists' conquest of social housing. This verticalization did not entail fresh direct investment in the sector but only the establishment of an extra superstructure to control a phenomenon whose impact had previously been, above all, local. No new spending item is cited in the law, which was effectively a rearrangement of an already consolidated system.

Between 1935 and 1939, the new consortium completed just 13,700 houses, work on most of which had been begun before the constitution of the new body, providing accommodation for 75,000 people. In 1940, however, the Ministry of Corporations calculated that the new housing requirement in Italy amounted to at least 600,000 units a year.[13] As in other fields of the *res publica*, in social housing the Fascist regime merely renamed and assumed control of administrative structures that had come into being in Liberal Italy.

From the town planning point of view, the Fascists were much more interested in projects with a propaganda impact on the population, such as public buildings focusing, above all, on symbolic and ceremonial functions. The regime had an architectural style and a conception of urban space of its own, which it developed through modernization schemes and monument building.

A symbol of the construction of Fascist space was the massive redevelopment of entire Roman neighborhoods.[14] Geared more to the visibility of the regime than to the needs of the population, some measures such as the demolition of the Borgo quarter were radical and controversial.[15]

The situation in Italy remained an emergency even in the later years of Fascism, when state funds earmarked for housing were funnelled into projects such as the building of a whole new neighborhood, EUR, designed to host the 1942 World's Fair. The project, which was eventually only completed in the 1950s, was an expensive showcase for Mussolini's achievements. As the historian Guido Melis writes, "The EUR quarter, which sprang up in anticipation of the twentieth anniversary of the regime, represented the apogee of the deliberate construction of a scenario."[16] It was not a place of public life but the wing of a theatre where the regime and its narrative were to be put on display.

This method of making political use of urban planning also extended to projects for the building of new towns in areas where land reclamation schemes were underway. In this case too, the building of new houses was a direct function of political consensus-building strategies and had no significant impact on real housing needs. Even at the time, a great deal of criticism was leveled at the Fascists' poor management of the housing

problem, with Giuseppe Pagano, one of the leading rationalist architects of the period, famously
accusing the regime, to which he had initially
been close, of spending money only "for the
building of magnificent mountains of marble."[17]

These projects weighed heavily on the state
coffers but failed to meet the demand for housing of millions of Italians who, throughout
the twenty years of Fascist rule, either lived in
precarious conditions or emigrated. In 1942,
Amintore Fanfani, then a young economics pro-
fessor, wrote a study of poverty and its causes in
Italy in which he denounced the shameful living
conditions in many parts of the country, where
dirt and overcrowding were rife.[18] The chronic
lack of housing continued until the outbreak of
World War II, when, even as the Duce's projects
were grinding to a halt on account of the hostil-
ities, many people who did have a home lost it as
a result of Allied bombing. At the end of the war,
it was calculated that the conflict had destroyed
two million housing units and seriously damaged
another million.[19]

The housing emergency, which had been
aggravated by Mussolini's warmongering policy,
was addressed afresh at the end of the war. With
the progressive reorganization of the state apparatus, it was clear that one of the first problems
to attend to was the desperate housing situation. In 1949, a series of measures, contained in

Law 43,[20] produced an organic and coordinated national housing scheme at last. The new legislation provided for the constitution of a special institute within the larger Istituto Nazionale delle Assicurazioni, the National Insurance Institute: its job was to manage a seven-year investment plan, subsequently extended to continue until 1963, in order to meet the demand for low-cost housing and that of labor in the construction sector. The resulting I.N.A.-Casa, an organic public investment scheme, was implemented nationwide to create jobs in the sector and develop projects to solve the housing problem.

While it operated, from 1950 to 1962, the scheme led to 20,000 sites being launched for residential construction work and 350,000 families accommodated in decent homes. The operation also provided employment for 40,000 people every year.[21] The promotor of the scheme was Amintore Fanfani, who became a leading politician in the Christian Democrat party after the war. He was the man who implemented the lesson he had learned by analyzing the state of abandon of housing conditions in Italy under Fascism. The buildings erected after the war are still remembered today as the "*case Fanfani*," Fanfani's houses. Once the emergency was over, in the boom years of Italy's "economic miracle," management of the building of social housing was progressively transferred to the local level.

Mussolini and emergencies

If Mussolini and Fascism were inadequate builders, they were no better when it came to rebuilding.

Cyclical controversies have arisen about public action in the wake of the earthquakes that have scourged Italy in recent years, and images and messages have appeared in the social media comparing the response of today's governments to the one that Mussolini would have had. This revisionist comparison is, naturally enough, damning: the thesis is that, faced with catastrophes, the organizational capabilities of and, above all, the results achieved by the regime were incomparably better than those of any republican government.

For Fascism too had an opportunity to come to terms with a natural catastrophe whose impact on the population was devastating. On July 23, 1930, in fact, the Irpinia and Vulture areas, in Campania and Basilicata respectively, were hit by an earthquake. The combination of the quake and the poor quality of housing caused a death toll of 1,404 victims.

The story of the earthquake and the government's reactions is reconstructed in the historical data sets of the Istituto Nazionale di Geofisica e Vulcanologia, the National Institute of Geophysics and Vulcanology,[22] which collects not only the geophysical data of the quake but also institutional communications concerning the emergency and subsequent reconstruction.

The first legislative action after the event was the Royal Decree of August 3, 1930,[23] which acknowledged the systematic approach to the emergency adopted by the government: hence the suspension of local roof tax collection, a moratorium on property taxes and a grant to cover 40 percent of reconstruction costs (arts. 1-10), plus an allocation of 100 million lire for the emergency (art. 11), the tasking of reconstruction coordination work to civil engineers (arts. 12-17) and the granting of easy-term credit to the victims of the disaster (art. 18). These articles were followed by a series of others regulating the role of the various ministries in the emergency.

The local prefects immediately declared the decree insufficient for dealing with the emergency. According to experts, in fact, "in terms of destructiveness and scope, this earthquake is emerging as one of the greatest seismic events in the twentieth century."[24] For propaganda reasons, Mussolini immediately opposed the building of shacks to house the homeless, "advancing the justification that though they would have responded to immediate needs, they would have left unresolved the housing problem to which the government intended to provide a definitive solution with new spending."[25] The idea had been to address the emergency with the construction of thousands of new prefabricated homes, which would have represented a more stable and dignified solution for the earthquake victims.

The government's approach was driven by two necessities: on the one hand, a year on from the Great Crash of 1929, it had to seek to balance public finances, on the other, it had to show off the regime's much vaunted organizational capacities. The inadequacy of the state's response to the first great earthquake of the century, that of Messina in 1908, was still very much impressed in the public imagination, hence the decision not to build the temporary homes—even though this meant that the people affected had to live in tents for months—and to adopt a more definitive approach to the problem of housing them.

The building of the new houses, however, turned out to be an organizational fiasco due to the costs and difficulties involved in transporting the prefabricated parts, and with the first cold of winter Mussolini was forced under pressure from the local prefects to agree to the building of a thousand wood huts. Nine hundred and sixty-one of them were eventually built, bringing the total of new dwellings to 3,746. The cost, 68 million lire, the equivalent of 70 per cent of all the funds allocated by the emergency decree, was exorbitant. The funds were insufficient, the red tape embarrassing: tasked with granting easy-term reconstruction loans and duly supported by the state, one year on from the earthquake the Banco di Napoli had only completed a tiny portion of the relevant paperwork. The sum of a hundred million lire allocated in August 1930 was supplemented by 35 million in 1931,[26] as well as by guarantees for coverage of the loans the Banco di Napoli was struggling to release. The financial commitment amounted to a total of about 160 million lire. In its reports to Mussolini, the Fascist Ministry of Public Works described the figure as dramatically insufficient. A total of 7,000 new prefabricated homes were constructed, a laughable number for local areas in which 35-40 percent—and in some places 70 percent—of residential property had been so badly damaged as to be uninhabitable. The Avellino provincial authority alone reported 100,000 homeless people.[27] The only real solution to the problems caused by the earthquake following the demolition of the tent cities a few months after the event was emigration. A large portion of the population of Irpinia and Vulture did not return to their places of origin but either went abroad or to more developed areas of the country.

"But He was a great urban planner!"

Was the Duce a road builder?

Another point some dwell on to underline the Fascists' building capabilities is that "it gave Italy a modern road network." That Italy had an infrastructure problem was well-known and it had dragged on since unification: the road network, for example, was in pitiful condition. It was the government of Giovanni Giolitti (1920-21) and that of his successor Ivanoe Bonomi (1921)[*] that launched an initial infrastructure building scheme. Expensive but necessary, it met, however, with firm opposition from some of the right-wing political formations of the time. They argued that the cost was unjustified and designed to favor the construction activities of workers' cooperatives, some of whose sites were boycotted and sabotaged. The fiercest opponent of the scheme was precisely Mussolini's Fascist Party. In the meantime, the development of efficient communications was left to private initiative.

The man who came up with the idea for the autostrada, or freeway, in Italy was an engineer,

---

[*] Giovanni Giolitti (1842-1928), a leader of the Historical Left, was Prime Minister of Italy five times between 1892 and 1921. (translator's note)

Ivanoe Bonomi (1873 –1951), Italian statesman who became Prime Minister of Italy on 1921 when Giolitti resigned. He had previously been Minister of War in Giolitti's cabinet. (translator's note)

Piero Puricelli. It was he who had the brainwave of building a network of roads with fast-flowing traffic whose cost would be amortized by the payment of tolls.[28] In 1921, he succeeded in having his plan for a road for motor vehicles linking Milan to Varese and the Lombardy lakes approved as a project of public utility, even though it had begun as a private entrepreneurial experiment. The first section of Puricelli's new autostrada was inaugurated on September 23, 1923, when Mussolini's government had only been in office for a year.

Having taken power, the Fascists dusted off Giolitti's infrastructure dossier, while at the same time embracing Puricelli's ideas and allowing him to establish a publicly-backed private company to initiate a series of projects for a new network of *autostrade*, or freeways. The plan was ambitious, the funding insufficient. The first sections, such as Bergamo-Milan and Naples-Pompei, were followed by others, less remunerative but geared more to the public interest, which wreaked havoc on the coffers of roadbuilding companies and slowed down the "Fascist revolution on wheels."

Fewer than ten sections with an average length of about seventy kilometers were opened between 1924 and 1935. They were ultimately more a source of pride for the regime than a project of public utility. Suffice it to think that when the first section of the Milan-Lakes was inaugurated, there were only 78,262 motor vehicles on Italian roads.[29] The saga of Italy's great autostrada projects—most of which were never to leave the drawing board—came to an end in 1935 when the invasion of Ethiopia sent the cost of fuel rocketing. The dream of cars for everybody that had been toyed with by the Fascists and some of their major private sponsors—Giovanni Agnelli's FIAT, for example—thus remained a pipe dream.

The freeway network put in place by Puricelli, though state-funded, continued to lose money. Puricelli's own company had to be bailed out by the newborn Istituto per la Ricostruzione Industriale (Institute for Industrial Reconstruction), a bargain deal for Puricelli himself, who pocketed 500 million lire from the sale of the business, plus 42 million to cover his personal debts.[30] The public money spent to salvage the image of freeways as an Italian engineering feat was effectively diverted from less high-sounding but more useful investments, such as those for repairs to the regular main roads that were the cornerstone of commercial traffic in the country.

As in other cases, the problem of road infrastructure was solved only after the gruesome end of the Fascist regime and republican Italy's economic new beginning. The 1950s were the years of the real Italian transportation revolution, thanks to the decision to invest in the building of a large-scale nationwide network of toll auto-stradas and, at the same time, to incentivize the automotive industry and road haulage, which became the backbone of the Italian economic miracle.[31]

CHAPTER 4

Mussolini the Man of Law

Was the *Duce* an upright defender of justice?

One of the biggest myths doing the rounds about Fascism in Italy is that, notwithstanding all its corruption and abuse of power, typical of any totalitarian regime, it and Mussolini in particular represented a parenthesis of honesty and moral rectitude in the history of the political life of Italy. This is the kind of fake news that flourishes, of course, when comparisons are made with the political class of republican Italy: people who look back nostalgically to *Il Duce* juxtapose the alleged thieves and criminals who hog the stage today with a man who they see as having been an enlightened, uncorruptible statesman, whose only flaw was arguably that of punishing wrongdoers too harshly. However, such upright, almost austere conduct has no basis in history.

But before addressing such a vast, complex subject, it is important to clarify the difference between the concept of the rule of law and that of justice. For if justice is bound up with values and principles that transcend the field of law and spill over into morality, the rule of law is, more simply, observance of the laws in force. From this point of view, it is evident that, as a totalitarian movement that destroyed individual freedoms, Fascism was, by definition, unjust. There is little point in speaking about a relationship with justice in the case of a liberticidal regime that held onto power by force. Here I speak instead of the relationship between Fascism and the system of laws that regulated the country, and that the Fascists helped in part to write.

The relationship between the rule of law and Fascism was checkered and changed with time. Suspicions of dubious morality built up around Mussolini and sullied his public image right from the beginning. The first suspicious episode in the *Duce*'s political career dates from before World War I in 1914 when as editor of *Avanti!** he passed from neutralism to interventionism, from being opposed to Italy's entry in the war to promoting it in the space of few months. The speed and scope of the volte-face astonished many. In 1938, from his exile in France, the Italian historian and writer Angelo Tasca wrote in his

---

* *Avanti!* (Forward), founded on December 25, 1896, was the official daily newspaper of the Italian Socialist Party. It now exists solely online. (translator's note)

Nascita e avvento del fascismo [The Birth and Advent of Fascism] that, "This about-turn is perceived by the militants and workers who had followed him with blind faith as a betrayal. In the self-proclaimed country of Machiavelli, it dug an unbridgeable furrow between Mussolini and the working class."[1]

Mussolini's detractors accused him of selling out to the warmongers' cause for money. He was outraged by the accusation and always denied it, while at the same time managing to found a new daily newspaper, *Popolo d'Italia*, with sizable start-up capital. As the historian Spencer Di Scala recalls, Mussolini "achieved the feat [of founding a new paper], but the unclear origin of the funding, part of which supplied by industrialists keen to profiteer from the war, provoked the hostility of his comrades."[2] From then on, Mussolini was always accused of being a traitor and a crook by his former comrades on the socialist left.[3]

At the end of the war, when Mussolini tried to attract the masses of veterans disappointed by its outcome, the Fascist movement immediately came out in favor of radical upheaval in the Italian political scene. In 1919, in what was dubbed the San Sepolcro manifesto, the Fascists presented themselves as "an anti-party to mobilize veterans outside the traditional parties [...] The Fascists despised parliament and the liberal mentality, extolled the activism of minority groups who practiced violence and street demonstrations to support Italy's territorial claims and fight Bolshevism and the Socialist Party."[4]

The main occupation of the Fascist *squadre*, or action squads, in that period was to engage striking workers in bloody street battles, to destroy rival newspaper and trade union offices, and to attempt to gain credit as an autonomous armed force in the post-war chaos. It was anything but a phenomenon associated with the concepts of the rule of law protected by the constitutional and democratic order.

The Fascists were subversives, most of whom with a republican leaning, who engaged in a declaredly minority struggle. In fact, their political message was rejected that same year by the electorate, who punished the Fascist manifesto at the polling stations, leaving Mussolini and his followers without a seat in the Chamber of Deputies.[5] The electoral setback expedited the movement's metamorphosis into a political movement, an expression of order and conservation.

To conquer power, the Fascists needed to project a more reassuring image. This is why the *squadristi*, the action squad members, embarked on a systematic war on the left, taking sides with factory bosses and farmers and violently putting an end to strikes and demonstrations. As a result of this change of tack, Mussolini managed to win the support of the industrial and agrarian bourgeoisie, who saw the Blackshirts as low-cost militias which they could use to impose their will. Thanks to this new act of opportunism, consensus for Mussolini's movement, now a political party, grew considerably.

The Fascists had always been given to street violence, but now it was using that violence to "restore the rule of law" wherever it was lacking. This provided the pretext to proceed with the systematic elimination of their political opponents and impose their presence on the public stage. That was how the Fascists styled themselves as the party of legality. Though the paradox of a party trying to impose the rule of law through illegal means was not lost on many people, this did not prevent the Blackshirts from assuming the role of "legalizers" of Italian social life. Many did rise up against this glaring contradiction, however: in July 1921, when the left attempted for one last time to use strikes as a weapon to halt the march of the Fascists, who called for calm while at the same time bludgeoning their opponents in the streets, the workers' anti-Fascist demonstrations took the name of "legalitarian strikes."[6] But this did not stop the Fascists from setting themselves up as defenders of the law.

"The *Duce* put crooks in jail!"

Right from the outset, strict respect for the rules was not routine practice for Mussolini and his followers; nonetheless it morphed into a strong and effective pretext for propaganda. One of the Fascist hobby horses in those years was the need for the country to free itself from the political system of Liberal Italy, which they deemed corrupt insofar as it was not only old and decrepit but also dishonest and parasitic. The political life of Liberal Italy had often been shaken by scandals that had brought to light illicit earnings and misuse of public funds. The fact that the Fascists could come across as the cleaners of the system, as the new wave advancing and sweeping away everything that was old and unsound, was an essential component of the public image they wished to project.

Matteotti and Fascist honesty

Once they had conquered power, their aura as the government that respected the rule of law was a leitmotiv of the proclamations of the *Duce* and his ministers, who highlighted comparisons with the past whenever possible. This is probably why the first scandal of the Fascist era was hushed up with unprecedented brutality. It was simply impossible for the "new government" whose job was to renew Italy to trip over a banal kickback scandal in its second year in office.

The Socialist Giacomo Matteotti was an awkward figure for Mussolini's government to deal with from a number of points of view. Not only was he an incorruptible defender of the rule of law, much devoted to his role as an institutional opponent of Fascism, he was also an expert on budget policies and economic affairs. He was attacked on more than one occasion by *squadristi* during his parliamentary mandates, but this did not placate his attacks on Fascism as a political movement and as a government party, precisely because he saw it as not only violent but also corrupt and incapable. The *Corriere della Sera* journalist Carlo Silvestri[7] recalls that Matteotti was "a man who read the government budget as I would read a novel. And from his reading, Matteotti had come to hair-raising conclusions about some of the expenditure items, the slipshod accounting and so on."[8]

In spring 1924, as a member of the Chamber of Deputies Budget Committee, Matteotti had pointed out not so much the disorder in the accounts as the fact that the figures presented by the government had been deliberately altered: "From the figures anticipated by the premier, it transpired that the balanced budget that the government officially submitted to parliament and the sovereign on the occasion of the opening of the legislature, was a fake, whereas the real one, which envisaged a deficit of two billion lire, was the one the government was trying to have passed by the general budget committee."⁹

The danger that an anti-Fascist like Matteotti represented lay precisely in his ability to investigate: The Socialist deputy did not confine himself to denouncing the violence of the *squadrismo* which, at this point, the new prime minister, Mussolini, was simply dismissing with a shrug of the shoulders. On the committee, he opposed the government, exposing its accounting frauds and holding it to account for its shortcomings and trickery, which were altogether similar to those of the much-hated liberal period the Fascists were intent on erasing. Matteotti thus represented a dual danger for the Fascist government. Not only did he continue to protest Fascist violence, he also sought to prove that Mussolini's was a party of swindlers, equal to if not worse than the ones that had preceded it. If, in a certain sense, the Fascists were able to boast about their violence and *menefreghismo*, their couldn't-give-a-damn attitude, the charge of dishonesty would probably have been hard to digest for public opinion, which was demanding change.

Basing themselves on contemporary accounts, many historians argue that the murder of Giacomo Matteotti was a political and economic crime, in the sense that the intention was to silence the Socialist deputy in order to prevent him from destroying the Fascists' public image by showing them up as a gang of crooks getting rich quick on the state payroll. Pietro Nenni, a socialist politician opposed to the regime, recalls that, "the day after he was assassinated, Matteotti was due to speak to the Chamber of Deputies about the provisional budget and, without indulging in personalist scandal-mongering, he intended to attack the policy of De Stefani [then Mussolini's finance minister] and draw the country's attention to the characters who had got rich too quick in the shadow of Palazzo Chigi and the Palazzo del Viminale* and a level of corruption identical to the one that had characterised the Second French Empire."[10]

More specifically, it seems that the scandal involved kickbacks paid to a number of Fascist *gerarchi*, local Fascist Party leaders, by the Sinclair Oil corporation for the right to exploit potential oil reserves in the Po Valley and Sicily. The *Duce*'s brother Arnaldo Mussolini appears to be among those involved.[11] Over the years, many unconfirmed reports have emerged about the Matteotti murder.

---

* Palazzo Chigi, the Chigi Palace, is a former patrician residence in Rome, which now serves as the seat of the Italian Council of Ministers and since 1961 has been the official residence of the Prime Minister. Situated on the Viminal Hill in Rome, the Palazzo del Viminale has been the seat of the Italian Ministry of the Interior since 1925. Until 1961 it was also the official residence of the Prime Minister. (translator's note)

As Mauro Canali writes, "Aldo Gibelli, the *Corriere Italiano* accountant, let slip a number of serious indiscretions which were pounced on by the Communist deputy Ezio Riboldi. Gibelli had confided to acquaintances of his that he knew for a fact that Matteotti had been kidnapped because he was believed to be in possession of a document regarding the Sinclair agreement that proved that it was reached on the condition of the payment of six hefty bribes to as many leading members of the Fascist government."[12] The kidnapping and murder of the Socialist deputy on June 10, 1924, nipped any possibility of the scandal bursting in the bud.

The myth of Fascist purity spawned the paradox whereby a crime caused by the violence of a few rowdy Fascists was thought to be preferable to a crime resulting from the mafia-style desire to silence a critical voice that would have shown the world the regime's true nature: more that of a criminal association than a political party.

Renzo De Felice, albeit without having the latest studies at his disposal, was very clear about what he thought about the Fascist system. He wrote that, "There can be no doubt that a murky world of speculation lurked in the shadow of the government,"[13] and also that, "So, even if it still cannot be documented today [the citation is taken from the 1995 edition of the book], I do not believe that the theory that there may have been a speculative side to the crime can be confined to the realm of imagination: too many signs lead to this conclusion."[14]

Leaving aside the legal implications that the uncovering of the Sinclair Oil scandal might have had, what is striking is that the regime threw off its mask before parliament and public opinion with Mussolini's famous speech of January 3, 1925, in which he himself assumed the "political, moral and historical responsibility for all that has happened."[15] One of the most significant implications of the speech was Mussolini's admission that violent conduct was not an unfortunate corollary of the way in which the Fascists had chosen to take power, but part of an organic strategy designed to raise the bar of confrontation by making illegal Fascist violence a necessity. It was a shrewd move: Mussolini was not only aware of the violence, he was also responsible for it. This contradictory behavior is enough on its own to reveal the instrumental nature of the Fascists' relationship with the rule of law. The law had to be abided by if it served to repress opponents and nonconformists, ignored if it got in the way of the aims of the regime. And if, finally, it clashed too obviously with the *Duce*'s ambitions, it had to be rewritten.

To a certain extent, defenders of Fascism past and present have sought to play down this casual use of moral categories, ascribing it to the need to take power by any means in order to be able to really change things. It was merely a matter of adopting any method available, lawful but above all unlawful, to reach the control room and lead the rebirth of the country from there. This turbulent beginning would be followed by twenty years of fairness and legality.

Leaving aside for the moment the perils of the Machiavellian argument that the end justified the means, if we analyze the behavior of the Fascist movement once it had established itself as a regime and a government, we see that its relationship with the rule of law was, to say the least, rocky.

When they consolidated their power, it became clear that managing the public apparatus made Fascists just as thievish as their predecessors. Corruption was widespread, especially among the rank and file of the party, which as the years went by became a parasite of the apparatus itself. The regime, in short, put in place a nationwide system of patronage, siphoning off public wealth and using it to bankroll the party and its members.

One episode already mentioned above was the official awarding of entire public budgetary components to friendly bodies, as was the case of the involvement of the Opera Nazionale Combattenti in land reclamation schemes, and of the 1939 law on the employment of *squadristi* in state enterprises. It was a vicious circle in which the Fascists drained the public coffers to increase their strength and thus maintain power. But the problem of legality also involved individuals, who barefacedly abused their positions of power to demand kickbacks and grant favors. As Paul Corner writes about Roberto Farinacci, the Fascist Party leader in Cremona, "Despite his dubious professional credentials, as a lawyer Roberto Farinacci was able to demand and receive six-figure fees for interventions in legal cases in which he used his political clout to fix sentences."[16]

Mussolini obviously knew what was going on. As De Felice writes, "Judging from the way Mussolini talked, his moral intransigence was absolute [...] But, in reality, he applied the rule only to the small fry, when condemnation of minor cases was unlikely to provoke scandal and, indeed, when he thought punishing the culprits might even benefit the regime [...] His behaviour was entirely different in more serious cases involving figures in the public eye that would provoke scandal."[17]

Some episodes did reach public opinion despite the censorship. The example of the funds earmarked for the Irpinia and Vulture earthquake in 1930 was mentioned above. During reconstruction, prefects in situ complained that the funds, though insufficient anyway, had been dissipated in a thousand little streams before reaching their destination. The cost of building "quake-proof" houses, for example, rose to double that estimated. The same was true of supplies to the armed forces: one of the reasons why the Italian army was dramatically unprepared for war was that the already paltry funds set aside for modernization were eaten up in bribes and embezzlement.

That Mussolini was aware of the phenomenon is attested by the reports of auditing bodies, by the trials that, with the *Duce*'s consent, were occasionally held against supporters of the regime, and even by his own personal complaints. Nonetheless, even when the magistrature did investigate the misdemeanours of the *gerarchi*, the local party leaders, "the watchword was always to avoid scandals that might discredit the party in the eyes of the people."[18]

One of the jobs of the infamous OVRA (Organizzazioni di Vigilanza e Repressione dell'Antifascismo), the Fascist political police, was to keep watch and spy on these *gerarchi* and other people close to the *Duce* in order to ensure close control of their political tendencies, reporting any wrongdoings or illegal behaviour."[19] The OVRA's immense archive, which Mussolini kept in his private study,[20] survived the war and offers a depressing view of a cross-section of his clan. It includes information about everything from their misappropriation of public money to their private vices and shows that the *Duce*'s cronies capitalized in every way on their proximity to power. From the perversions of party cadre such as Pavolini and Starace to the company kept by the *Duce*'s eldest daughter Edda, the picture that emerges from the police files is excruciating.

Mussolini was well-acquainted with the vices of single individuals but never punished them with any great resolve. The purpose of the files was essentially to collect ammunition to blackmail internal opponents, not to rid the state apparatus of rotten apples. The same system was later adopted as routine practice by most party officials.[21] By basing itself on the internal investigations commissioned by Mussolini himself, Fascism was thus a system for misappropriating wealth for personal ends.

Mussolini himself was very attentive to his own personal economic well-being and to that of his blood relations. He was careful to place friends and relatives in important positions. The most glaring example was that of Galeazzo Ciano, who became Foreign Minister and the regime's second-in-command simply because his father, Costanzo Ciano, was one of the *Duce*'s most faithful followers, and because he was husband to the *Duce*'s daughter. Over the years, Mussolini's extended clan came to dominate the country's highest authorities. The *Duce* himself admitted as much in his infamous address following the Matteotti murder on January 3, 1925: "If Fascism has been a criminal association, the responsibility for this is mine!"[22]

There are still those who defend Mussolini's image, admitting that the Fascist movement was corrupt but that its *Duce* was not: even if some of the regime's men were beneath contempt, their leader was free from all blame. The idea of Mussolini as an ascetic figure, allergic to luxury, almost poor, was disseminated for the first time by Fascist propaganda in an attempt to build the image of a disinterested dictator devoted exclusively to his subjects. It is true that Mussolini never cashed his salary as head of state, donating it instead to charity. In a clearly symbolic gesture, he always declared that he earned a living through his salary as a journalist and for the articles he wrote, especially for the foreign press, even when he was Prime Minister.

One might question whether the man who was absolute dictator of a whole nation for twenty years had a real need for ready cash, yet there are still people today who are blinded by the effects of the propaganda of the time. Though he never spent the salary due to him as the head of the government, he was at the same time perfectly willing to accept the gifts and perks that arose from his position. On August 31, 1936, for example, the Senate of the Kingdom of Italy decided to donate Mussolini a sum for the "celebration of the foundation of the Empire" without recording the amount in its books. On June 11, 1938 it made him a second donation, this time for one million lire (the total amount of the emoluments of all the senators that year was 932,000 lire).[23] The citizenry of Forlì restored the Rocca delle Caminate castle and gave it to him. If in the Romagna region he owned a modest villa, when he was in Rome he resided with his family at the splendid Villa Torlonia, paying a symbolic rent of one lira a year. He spent his holidays on the royal estate of Castel Porziano, a long stretch of coastline near Rome, where the President of the Republic now takes his vacations.[24]

With all the property and means of the State at his disposal, giving up his premier's emoluments would not appear to be a major sacrifice. When he fled for the last time in April 1945, Mussolini did not hesitate to take money and gold from the coffers of the Bank of Italy for himself and his most faithful cronies in a bid to secure safety. The last act of a man who had always had a somewhat conflictual relationship with the rule of law was, de facto, to appropriate public money and wealth to pay for his own escape.[25]

Did Fascism defeat the mafia?

Another question that unfolds around the vast subject of Mussolini's presumed legality is that of the efficacy of Fascist justice. If it is undeniable that the regime attacked individual liberties as soon as it could, some still argue that through his actions the *Duce* succeeded in imposing the rule of law in many areas of the country. The main argument favoring this counter-narrative is that Fascism was supposedly the only system of government capable of defeating the mafia. This argument is deliberately framed to impress by setting the imaginary victories of the past against the obvious difficulties, failures and even the conniving of the republican governments on the issue ever since.

When the Fascists took power the mafia was a firmly rooted phenomenon in Sicily, where all the measures taken by the Liberal governments after Italian unification had proved largely ineffective in combating the phenomenon.[26] Like many of the problems endemic to Italian society, the fight against the mafia also became the object of a Fascist propaganda campaign devised to demonstrate that, in this field too, the *Duce* would succeed where other governments had failed.

"He defeated the mafia; the people ruling today are all mafiosi."

After World War I, agricultural workers' rights movements in Sicily sparked unrest in the population at large. Here as elsewhere central government appeared somewhat indifferent to the grievances of the working classes: the large landowners had long built relations of power and patronage with many members of the Liberal majorities in Rome. Moreover, many of the Sicilian deputies and senators were the very *latifondisti*, or landowners, who were preventing natural development of the island.

In the wake of the land movements in Northern Italy, in 1921, however, a point was scored in favor of free access to land by the people who worked it. With the Royal Decree of December 15, 1921,[27] in fact, Ivanoe Bonomi's Liberal government approved the concession of uncultivated land to the peasant consortia that had applied for it. It was a heavy blow to the power of the large landowners and the mafiosi who supported them. After all, discretional possession and control of the land were two cornerstones of the whole mafia system.

When he was still one of the many northern politicians foraging for votes on the island,

Mussolini presented himself in Sicily as the champion of order and discipline. Taking a stance characterized by force and the desire to fight chaos—especially where protests for the enforcement of the new law on land occupation were seen as chaos—Mussolini immediately became popular among Sicilian *latifondisti*, whose main concern was to placate peasants clamoring for bread and rights. With their demands for land and reforms, agricultural workers, who were united in unions and cooperatives, had been the real opponents of the mafia power system from the early twentieth century. But it was precisely against this popular movement to liberate the island from criminality that the first Sicilian Fascists railed.

The accusation was the same as the one levelled in the case of *squadrista* expeditions into the countryside of the lower Po Valley, where movements of farm laborers and peasants were accused of Bolshevism and being eager to stoke revolution. In short, gangs of Fascist thugs, identical to the mafia's own rank-and-file hoods, became the armed branch of the *latifondisti*. The period between 1921 and 1923 thus saw a succession of Fascist squad assaults on socialist militants, the burning down of party branch offices, and violence during trade union demonstrations.

When they finally took power, the Fascists' first decision on this issue was, not coincidentally, the repeal of the concession of land to the peasant cooperatives on January 11, 1923.[28] The most effective tool for fighting the mafia ever implemented until then—namely the law providing for the progressive demolition of the landed estate system—was thus erased by Mussolini just three months after his appointment as Prime Minister. Insofar as the mafia was an alliance between local interests and strict control of the local lands, it is possible to say that the Fascist regime was a good friend of the Sicilian system that lived and did business with the mafia right from the beginning.

If anything, at first, it was the mafia itself that did not side openly with the Fascists. Some historians have pointed out that many leading mafiosi made an error of judgment by sticking with the old Italian political parties, such as the Liberals, and thereby provoking Mussolini's "vendetta."[29]

In his *Storia della Mafia*,[30] Salvatore Lupo offers a good description of this split between the old landowning aristocracy, which continued for some time to defend its bonds with the parties of Liberal Italy, and those who we might define as "secessionists," new mafiosi who chose to follow the Fascist wave and eventually came out on top as winners. Indeed, the regime served as a safety valve for rank-and-file mafiosi, who otherwise would not have found alternative employment: "[...] The Blackshirt movement provided discontented Mafiosi and would-be *Mafiosi* with a wonderful opportunity for using the state apparatus to supplant their established rivals, and thus intensified the internal tensions of *Mafia*."[31]

Once in power, however, the Fascists decided to turn the struggle against the mafia into a propaganda banner: the *Duce* was sure to succeed where others before him had failed. For Fascist rhetoric, the mafia, which had stayed alive thanks to the state's relative inability to control its own territory, was thus a foe to be vanquished. This is why, following a fact-finding journey to the island, it was Mussolini himself who, on October 23, 1925, dispatched Cesare Mori to be prefect of Palermo.[32]

Born in Pavia, Mori was an institutional figure who climbed the ladder in the final years of Liberal Italy, and as prefect of Bologna in 1921, forcefully defended the city against Fascist violence.[33] He worked in a determined way, and using much propaganda, to eradicate the mafia problem from Sicily. His system of hardline counteraction verged on brutality and brought to Sicily a state of emergency that nipped manifestations of mafia violence in the bud. Some mafiosi ended up in jail or in internal exile. Thanks to this battle and, above all, the way in which his actions were reported in the press, in the second half of the 1920s Mori became one of the state's most prominent figures, and his popularity sometimes obscured Mussolini's own. The problem of this narrative, however, lay in the fact that, in the eyes of public opinion, the prefect was a functionary who could not be entirely assimilated into the new wave of Fascists that had invested the institutions. Mori was hard to control and as he piled up successes, he risked casting a shadow over the regime.

Hence, even as Mori was publicly demanding greater powers to fight the mafia and becoming Italy's hero of the rule of law, in 1929, Mussolini decided to declare that the mafia in Sicily had been defeated. He thanked Mori for his contribution and told him he had reached retirement age—he was only 57. When the prefect asked for his retirement to be postponed, his request was rejected.[34]

Judging from the official crime statistics, between 1924 and 1943 mafia crimes did fall in Sicily and virtually disappeared from 1929 on. How did the regime achieve such an outstanding statistical result? The answer is simple: during the dictatorship public reporting of mafia crimes was banned. The newspapers stopped speaking about them and public opinion was no longer informed about episodes of violence.

At the same time, common violent crime increased with murders being dismissed as crimes of honor and the pocketing of protection money as simple theft. The mafia was not so much eliminated by Fascism as "silenced," not only in the sense that it was prevented from acting openly but also that its operations were not investigated. Worse still, they were hushed up. As Enzo Ciconte has pointed out, "the mafia was not defeated because, contrary to what was thought, it was a much more complex phenomenon that could not be addressed and resolved with repressive action, no matter how large-scale that action was. [...] The mafia continued to live on even after Mori."[35]

In 1943, the Allied liberation of Sicily and the collapse of the Fascist regime on the island created a power vacuum in which the mafia system became visible again in all its virulence. The mafia's balance of power, its contacts and even its structure became active and dynamic again as soon as Mussolini fell—in other words, when investigations were resumed into mafia crimes, which began to be called by their real name again.

According to one public narrative, many mafia bosses who had sought shelter in the United States during the Fascist period returned to Sicily when it came to an end. The underlying idea is that the Allies brought the mafia back to the island and thereby thwarted Mussolini's previous efforts. It is true that many influential names in the mafia returned to Sicily and, indeed, were reinstated in their positions of power by the

Allied Forces. But it is precisely the ease with which they regained control and began to lord it again—twenty years after Fascism had declared war on the mafia and fourteen years after its alleged defeat by the regime—that demonstrates how, in reality, the organization had never left Sicily, either as a means for controlling local lands or as a structure for ruling society.

CHAPTER 5

Mussolini the Economist

Did the *Duce* raise the Italian economy to its highest point?

Under Mussolini, Italians were richer than they are today. This assertion is sometimes to be found in the social media, used especially to compare the Italian economic crisis of recent years with the memory of a prosperous, happy past. The basic thesis of many online polemicists is that more than seventy years of democracy have failed to improve or maintain the economic—and welfare—standards they ascribe to the Fascist period.

It would appear that in the *Duce*'s day, things "went better" from an economic point of view. It is hard to say what this loud statement really means. There are a great many aspects to be taken into account if we are to attempt a sensible comparison between past and present. To have a clearer picture, it might be useful to consider the situation Italy was in at the advent of the Fascist dictatorship, to evaluate the points of departure and arrival of a regime that intervened in the country's economic affairs a lot.

"We were all richer!"

The Italian economy before Mussolini

When Benito Mussolini conquered power by force in 1922, Liberal Italy was prey to the post-war economic crisis. The extreme difficulty involved in reconverting an entire wartime economy for peacetime purposes, the demobilization and sudden return of four million soldiers from the front, a world economy crippled by the destruction of whole consumer markets—these were the problems that Italian governments had to grapple with after 1918.

Due to spending on the war, public debt had exploded from 15,766 lire in 1914-15 to 92,857 million lire in 1921-22, and this 429 percent increase had already raised the public debt-to-GDP ratio to 125 percent in 1920.[1] In order to come to terms with this perilous financial situation, Liberal governments undertook a set of economic initiatives that began to bear fruit from the 1921-22 fiscal year. At the same time, they began to negotiate further deferment of the repayment of the war debt contracted with the United States and Great Britain, which together held 99 percent of it,[2] to ensure that the state apparatus would not be squeezed by lack of resources. It was in this period that the total debt began to fall. As the historian and anti-Fascist Gaetano Salvemini sums up, "In 1922, hence before the March on Rome, a situation was achieved in which it was possible to halt and pare down the growth of the public debt."[3]

The budget squeeze that befell an Italy already demoralized by the clashes of the so-called "Red Biennium" (1919 and 1920, when Italy seemed on the verge of revolution) was effective but also brutal. It was a policy of austerity so harsh that it undermined the relationship between active society and the institutions, and the Fascists inevitably capitalized on this when it rose to power.

The Fascists take charge of the economy

The way out of the crisis was slow and laborious. Italy, a country that was already strongly export-oriented, without raw materials and with a positively modest domestic market, had to struggle to get back on its feet in a period of general difficulty for the world economy. From the beginning, the policies undertaken by the new Mussolini government failed to improve the situation, and throughout the 1920s Fascist Italy's GDP never managed to catch up with global recovery. One of the country's paradoxes was precisely that: though it had won the war, the growth rate of its economy was comparable to that of the losers, not that of the winners.

Mussolini, admittedly, did inherit some of the structural problems of the liberal economic system, such as exasperating red tape and inadequate infrastructure, but during his twenty-year dictatorship he nonetheless ended up aggravating these flaws and exacerbating endemic problems. The united Italy of the second half of the nineteenth century had followed the classic trajectory of developing countries, seeking to couple the train of advanced economies. This meant uneven development, industrial production localized only in certain districts, widespread poverty, and very cheap labor costs. But until the early years of the Mussolini government, the Italian economy was described as being "in convergence" with other European economies. Once the exceptional circumstances of the post-war period had been overcome, the situation was one of promising expansion. After three years in government, in 1925, a much-trumpeted balanced budget became one of the feathers in the cap of early Fascist economic policy. After years of rash economic management in which public debt had been allowed to push the state coffers into the red, in just two years Mussolini was able to declare that the state budget had been balanced.

This balancing of the public accounts is another of the great hobby horses of the *Duce*'s admirers: not propaganda, they say, but the budget figures themselves are evidence of the regime's economic capabilities.

This is one of the pet subjects of today's keyboard revisionists who attack the deplorable state of the Italian public accounts since the crisis of 2008 and European interference in Italian economic policies. In the face of the present difficulties, the extreme right commonly emphasizes that the *Duce* succeeded where petty politicians fail. But the point is that a closer look at the statistical archives of the public accounts shows that the balanced budget of 1925 was achieved not by Fascist good management but by the repayment of the major financial commitments contracted due to war debts.

It was the settlement of the hefty borrowings that had served to finance the war—partly with the money from the war reparations paid by defeated Germany—that made it possible to balance the budget. This fortunate coincidence was obviously exploited by the Fascists to boast about their superior administrative skills compared to those of the ministers of Liberal Italy, but even at the time many economists were critical of the way in which Mussolini unduly took credit for the achievement.

As early as 1922, economist and statistician Giorgio Mortara was writing in a public finance report that if no amendments were made to economic policies, the budget deficit would be eliminated in 1924.[4] In concrete terms, according to Mortara's calculations, Mussolini's early policies did not accelerate the balancing of the books but rather delayed it. In a letter to his colleague Pasquale D'Aroma on December 23, 1923, the future President of the Republic Luigi Einaudi, already an economist of international fame, even wrote that the budget had already been balanced, "in 1922-23, though those sterling morons Facta and C. didn't realize it [...]. In short, I say that the budget inherited from the war and after the war has already been balanced for two fiscal years (the last one and the current one); and if there is to be a deficit, then it will be a novelty with new causes that will have nothing to do with previous and present rulers."[5] In 1923, Giacomo Matteotti branded the whole budget balancing policy that the Fascists were boasting about as "a fairy tale for ignoramuses."[6]

Mussolini appointed the world-famous economist Alberto De Stefani as Minister of Finance in his first government. A *squadrista* and Fascist "of the first hour,"[7] De Stefani had very clear ideas about the needs of the Italian economy and did his utmost to implement them with almost military discipline. This extremely rigorous figure was a good fit for the propaganda that painted the new government as a determined promoter of change. In reality, De Stefani continued the policy of austerity initiated by the Liberals with unpopular choices, rebalancing "the accounts of the postal and railway administrations by increasing tariffs and cutting personnel [...] In 1923, 65,000 public employees were also laid off."[8] De Stefani's over-rigid policies against inflation eventually provoked a stock market crash and a financial crisis that engulfed the whole banking system.[9]

After taking credit for balancing the budget, however, Mussolini decided to abandon De Stefani's austerity policies and launched a more amenable collaboration with the captains of Italian industry, who had complained of the minister's excessive intransigence. After serving as the incorruptible face of the regime, De Stefani was dismissed from the government at the explicit behest of Confindustria, the National Employers' Association.[10]

From that year, in which, among other things, the first great Fascist economic reforms were set into motion, the phenomenon of the century-old rapprochement with the advanced economies was interrupted for the first time. This virtuous trend was not halted by exogenous factors or by the hardening of international economic conditions, which, if anything, constituted an aggravating circumstance. On the contrary, it was the regime's economic choices that were largely responsible for the economic slowdown. From the second half of the 1920s, the government launched a set of economic reforms largely inspired by the propaganda effect they would have on the country.

One of the most glaring examples was the so-called "Quota 90" (*Quota Novanta*) monetary revolution.[11] The name derives from an expression coined by Mussolini to describe his objective of pegging the exchange rate 90 lire against the pound sterling. For the Fascists, a "strong nation" needed a "strong currency." For the regime, being defined as "strong" was a token of prestige, irrespective of the adjective's connotations in macroeconomic field. The forced revaluation of the lira had inevitable consequences: the British currency, then the most stable in the world, was pegged to the price of gold by the so-called "gold standard."

In practice, imposing a fixed exchange rate against the pound meant preventing the value of the lira from reflecting the fundamentals of the national economy and maintaining a balance with the values of the world's currencies. When this battle was launched in 1926, the exchange rate was 155 lire for a pound sterling. The Italian currency had undergone huge devaluations in the wake of postwar turbulence and, set against the strong currencies of the period, revealed all the weaknesses of the Italian system. Making the lira lose value had been the quickest way of making goods competitive abroad, a step that was indispensable for the economic relaunch of a manufacturing country like Italy.

One of the measures adopted to help strengthen the lira was to cut the wages of almost all categories of workers.[12] This led to a drop in consumption and economic stagnation in Italy, even before the stock market crash of 1929. As the statistical archives of the Bank of Italy demonstrate, when the exchange rate of 88 lire to the pound was reached, in 1927—that is, when Mussolini's battle was seen as being won—the major industries close to the regime found themselves with a currency that made it easier to purchase raw materials abroad and pay wages cut by almost a fifth. However, most Italian workers found themselves with reduced wages and savings capacity. The first Fascist intervention in the economy thus made Italians not richer but poorer in terms of spending power, by an average of 15 percent.

This cut hit the working classes in particular and wage-earners in general—that is to say the country's weakest classes—who, among other things, had just been deprived of the right to strike and, as a result, had no legal means of holding government policy to account. Moreover, if wages fell immediately, the same was not true of the prices of consumer goods, as the economic historian Salvatore La Francesca pointed out in the 1970s: "Wages and salaries were cut by 10 to 20 percent in a situation that deprived workers of the right to strike and access to authentic trade union representation, with retail prices staying relatively stable. This trend was to continue in the years that followed."[13]

Placing the dynamics of Fascist economic policies in context, it is only fair to admit that the regime found itself ruling Italy in the middle of the greatest crisis of capitalism in the 20th century, a period of widespread difficulty which brought all the advanced economies to their knees. Any judgment on the effectiveness or otherwise of Mussolini's policies is possible only by comparing them with the methods and solutions implemented by the other countries involved and the very different ways and speed with which countries comparable to Italy emerged from the crisis.

In 1929 the Great Depression hit everyone hard: in Italy, which still had the economy of a developing country and was still suffering the after-effects of the Great War, the crash immediately overwhelmed banks, which brought the entire financial system down with them. The bottom fell out of the export-based industrial and manufacturing sectors, while those relying on the domestic market were, as we have seen, already in trouble on account of Fascist monetary policy.

IRI (Instituto per la Ricostruzione Industriale)

The most important of the measures taken by the government to address the crisis was its bailing-out of investment banks with public money. This was supplemented by the establishment of a body to take over and prop up all the industrial conglomerates that were struggling to stay on the market. The body in question, the Istituto per la Ricostruzione Industriale (Institute for Industrial Reconstruction, IRI), was founded in 1933.[14]

In reality, the measure was not a Fascist invention at all but rather the expansion of a public business support system designed in 1913 and activated in 1915 with the setting up of the Industrial Securities Finance Consortium or Consorzio per Sovvenzioni su Valori Industriali.[15] As the economic historian Rolf Petri points out, "The Great Crash was not the midwife of a baby born from nothing. The road had already been bending for some time in the direction of public financing and support to productive activities thanks to the widespread conviction, not only among Nittian technocrats,* 'that in order to complete the industrialization and modernization of the country it was necessary to massively mobilize savings into the right hands.'"[16]

At the outset, the foundation of IRI was a well-advised emergency measure insofar as it saved the country's industrial fabric from fraying

---

* Francesco Saverio Nitti (1868–1953) was an Italian politician and economist. A leader of the Italian Radical Party, he served as Prime Minister from June 1919 until May 1920. (translator's note)

altogether, but it was only intended as a provisional move. Given the ongoing crisis and, above all, grasping the strategic importance of having a dominant industrial conglomerate under direct state control, in 1937 the regime decided to make the institute permanent.[17] The law that governed the IRI illustrates the nature of the regime's choice: "Art. 1. The Institute for Industrial Reconstruction (IRI), a public company, has the job of providing unitary criteria for the efficient management of the interests within its pertinence, according to the economic policy directives of the Regime, as expressed by the competent corporations. Interests and assets which the state has no interest in preserving will be gradually liquidated."[18]

The aim of the institute was no longer to rescue companies in distress but to pursue the regime's economic policies. This de facto authorization to liquidate shareholdings that were "uninteresting for the State" released IRI from its role as a cushion for the industrial fabric and made it a state-owned corporation. IRI had to save many companies immediately, using public money: according to the institute's 1934 budget, just one year after its establishment, 21.4 percent of the capital of all Italian businesses was controlled directly or indirectly by IRI, which covered almost 15 percent of the Italian GDP on its own.[19]

The medium- to long-term impact of the birth of IRI is disputed: if at first there was consensus for its support of the economy, the industrial colossus that specialized in taking over floundering businesses subsequently became a formidable competitor for private entrepreneurs and a structure capable of changing the fate of entire productive sectors by itself. IRI was an important element in the construction of the corporatist economic system, the supposedly Italian third way between capitalism and socialism that sought to direct the economy according to the interests of the Fascist regime.

The Institute was maintained well into the republican era and was only liquidated once and for all in 2002. It is interesting to note how in its golden age in the 1960s and 1970s, many on the right recalled that IRI had been one of the *Duce*'s inventions. But when the colossus found itself in difficulties and became one of the symbols of the inefficiency of direct state intervention in the economy, this merit stopped being flaunted. Now that the body no longer exists and the memory of it is associated with *Tangentopoli*,* no one in the social media claims that IRI was an invention of Mussolini's anymore.

---

* *Tangentopoli* (Graftsville), the popular term for the scandal triggered by the nationwide *Mani pulite* (Clean Hands) judicial investigation into political corruption in Italy, which in the early 1990s led to the collapse of the so-called "First Republic," along with that of a number of political parties. (translator's note)

Alone against the world!

Another important Fascist economic policy—partly the fruit of an increasingly aggressive foreign policy—was so-called "autarchy," the production of everything the state needed within its own national boundaries. In a celebrated speech to the assembly of the National Council of Corporations on March 23, 1936, Mussolini declared the need to move to a new form of economic development that would allow the country to address its coming military challenges.[20]

The idea pursued by the regime was basically to build a self-sufficient economy free from the influences of the international market. This step, it was argued, would allow Italy to move freely on the international stage without fearing sanctions from other countries. This military conception of international relations clashed, however, with the reality of an economy based on manufacturing dependent on international trade to grow but which had no raw materials and whose small domestic consumer market was still depressed. Propaganda campaigns on the need for national production of goods were described as "battles" and organized like veritable military campaigns, with targets to hit and schedules to meet.

One of the most famous was the great "Battle for Grain." Grain production was one of the many sectors in which Italy was not self-sufficient and forced to import goods from other countries. The propaganda was non-stop and photographs of a bare-chested *Duce* threshing bales of grain to set a good example have gone down in history. Though there was an increase in grain production,[21] Italian wheat now had to compete with a global commodities market in which raw materials from the vast prairies of the United States and Canada cost much less, even if they were transported from across the ocean. For ordinary citizens, the first true fruit of autarchy was thus the fact that they were unable to enjoy the benefits of international trade, such as the drop in prices of agricultural produce.

"When the Duce was in power, the crisis disappeared and everyone lived well, there was cleanliness and order, and people stopped striking."

(signed, apparently, Mahatma Gandhi)

Depression before the Great Depression

The result of this mixture of cosmetic provisions and miscalculation was that the Italian economy was already weak going into 1929, when the Great Depression destroyed the growth prospects of Western countries. The decade of economic difficulties into which the capitalist powers plunged between 1929 and the outbreak of World War II was addressed by each with differing results. Percentage-wise, Italy was less hit by the financial crash, partly because from a financial point of view its economic system was decidedly less developed and vulnerable than others. There was, nonetheless, a further impact on incomes and it is interesting to see how the various countries emerged from the Depression.

If we take the income of Italians in 1929 as 100, on account of the crash it fell to a minimum of 93.1 in 1930 and 1931, then increased again to 110.7 in 1937, the best result since 1929, with an average growth of 1 per cent a year. Then in 1938 it dropped to 110.6. On the eve of the Second World War, the Italian economy had virtually come to a standstill.

Taking the value for 1929 as 100, Great Britain, whose economy was much more sensitive to the global turmoil caused by the Depression, dropped to 71.6 in 1930, but clawed its way back to 111.1 by 1938. France slipped to a minimum of 70.2 in 1934, before applying recovery policies that took it back to 153.1 in 1938, measured again against the 1929 index of 100.[22]

The Italian economy was hit less than others but was still slower to recover. Industrial production, for example, returned to pre-Depression levels only after 1937.[23] Within this general picture of extreme difficulty, the people who paid the greatest price were above all workers, whose average real wages had been cut and frozen for years. The real value of salaries eventually managed to grind back to 1928 levels only in 1938.[24] Italian labor had lost a decade.

These data offer a relatively clear answer to the question of whether the Fascists took the Italian economy to its highest levels ever. The answer is no. Indeed, the regime not only failed to address the world crisis with effective measures but also crippled any chance of recovery. The gap between an Italian's average income and that of the inhabitants of other developed European countries, which was already wide at the beginning of the dictatorship, grew even wider thanks to the policies of Mussolini's government.

It was not only poor decision-making that conditioned the Italian economy during the Fascist period; a set of political choices also left a mark on the national budget. For example, the Fascist government implemented a costly expansionist policy that led to an explosion of public spending in projects that drained resources from the budget. The occupation in Libya, the war on Ethiopia, mass participation in the Spanish Civil War, the invasion of Albania and then, of course, World War II bled massive resources from the state coffers. According to a study on public debt published by the Treasury Ministry, the cost of the Fascists' military adventures "was 5,275 billion current lire [...]. Note that the cost of these wars was about two thirds more than that of World War I and the conquest of Libya, while the GDP had increased by one third."[25]

Observing the data, the spending on these expansionist adventures did not excessively affect the public debt, which stayed at around 90 per cent of the GDP until the outbreak of World War II. But there is a reasonably easy explanation for the apparently good news that the regime had kept public debt under control: it had a hard time financing itself on international markets. Pursuing confrontational policies with countries like Great Britain, which held the monopoly of the international credit market, turned off the taps. This forced Mussolini to pursue international expansion with other forms of funding: he attempted to draw on the savings of Italians at an increasingly high cost by increasing the cost of servicing public debt;[26] he waived balancing of the budget and implementing unguaranteed economic policies; he cut services aimed at improving the living conditions of his own citizens—what today we would refer to as welfare; he raised taxes; and he dipped into the reserves of the Bank of Italy (that is to say, using the country's gold reserves, meant to ensure the economic stability of the state apparatus) for current expenditures.[27]

This latter move was particularly harmful for the stability of the Italian system. At the height of the Depression in the 1930s, it found itself trapped in the regime's monetary policy—when the Depression began, even the pound and the dollar had been devalued to give the British and American economies breathing space. The economy was depressed, taxes were higher, and costly and rash military adventures were funded by selling the "family jewels."

The Fascists succeeded nonetheless in turning their blunderings in their favor by laying the blame for difficulties on foreign countries. For example, the extraordinary collection of precious metals announced during the invasion of Ethiopia on December 18, 1935, pompously dubbed the day of "Gold to the Fatherland," was a success, with citizens donating directly 35.5 tons of gold and as many as 114 of silver.[28] People were convinced they were helping the government to withstand the siege of the western powers in the wake of Italy's colonial war. The wedding rings of Italians served instead to fill the coffers of the state, to offset the shortages caused by forced withdrawals of monies that had begun in 1930.[29]

These extraordinary collections failed, however, to restore the government reserves, the state of which remained precarious until the outbreak of World War II and fatally conditioned the way it was conducted. Speaking about the situation in Italy and the possibility of sustaining a war at Germany's side, Ciano reported in his diary that in February 1940 Mussolini feigned confidence with regard to the gold reserves, but also added that, "But the *Duce* does not add that during that time we consumed twelve billions in foreign securities and five billions in gold. Now our reserves have been reduced to one thousand four hundred miserable millions, and when these are gone, we shall have only our eyes to weep with."[30]

Italians richer than ever before?

The Fascist period was a difficult one for the Italian economy on account both of the international economic situation and of the national system's age-old structural problems. Yet virtually all the initiatives undertaken during the period only helped to make things worse.

Social inequality in particular increased under Fascism: the gap between the richest section of society and the poorest grew wider and the limited circle of the super-rich, most of whom were followers of Fascism, was countervailed by the great mass of the population, whose only alternative of a better life was emigration. This was a fiasco for a regime that claimed to be sensitive to issues such as justice and equality, and turned the nation's general well-being into a veritable propagandist cult.

Compared to today, the vast majority of Italians were poor and were no better off than in the liberal period. Purchasing power fell on account of monetary policies, while consumer goods grew scarcer and more expensive owing to the isolationist policies and the hostility of the capitalist powers. The decrease in the availability of goods was general and extended to food and beverages. Charting the course of the fight against hunger and malnutrition in Italy over the last two centuries, the economic historians Maria Sorrentino and Giovanni Vecchi argue that "the Fascist regime's autarchic and exchange rate policies are clearly correlated to a reduction in the average calories available to Italians, which translates to an increase in the percentage of the population that was inadequately fed."[31]

The comparison between the Italy of yesterday and Italy today, which often crops up in the arguments in defense of the Fascist period, is humiliating. Today the average Italian wage is about 90 percent that of an advanced European country such as France; in the 1930s, the average Italian wage was 33 percent of the French one and less than 20 percent of the British one. Moreover, in France and Britain not only was it possible to find imported coffee and tobacco on store shelves, there were also civil liberties, namely the right to vote, strike and protest. Though they are hard to monetize, these are the factors that ought to be taken into account when addressing subjects such as the well-being of a people, or when making comparisons with the "good old days."

CHAPTER 6

Mussolini the Feminist

Did the *Duce* improve the status of women in Italy?

The relationship between Italian totalitarianism and women has spawned many false beliefs. In this area, fake news is generally based on the premise that the Fascist regime was more open to women's rights than the regimes that preceded it and have followed it.

Reference to the presumed merits of Fascism is usually accompanied by controversy about the many problems Italian society still has to resolve on issues concerning sexism. For some polemicists in the social media, the *Duce*'s reign represented a happy parenthesis for women and their rights.

Setting out from the sad premise that the question of parity for women in Italy in terms of wages, positions and recognition is still a long way from being solved, the first thing to do to assess the regime's impact on women's rights is to establish what we mean by conducting a policy in favor of gender equality, especially considering the real social conditions that held sway in Italy in the early twentieth century.

The watershed for women's conditions in Italy in the first twenty years of the last century was the Great War. Even before 1915, an organized movement was fighting for the recognition of women's "active" and "passive"* electoral rights in the country. It was made up largely of educated members of the upper-middle classes, who fought for causes that were not widely shared or heard in a nation that had other problems to address, such as industrialization, literacy and poverty.

As Giulia Galeotti reminds us in her *Storia del voto alle donne in Italia* [History of the Women's Vote in Italy], "Italian suffragettes were, broadly speaking, establishment women, Mazzinian by allegiance and education, in some way tied to important figures of the time."[1] In other words, they were not a vast nor a representative group in society.

During World War I, the need to stand in for men who had been called to the front brought women to the foreground and irreversibly changed their role in society: working in factories and in essential services or finding themselves

---

* In Italy, there is a distinction between the "active" right to vote (i.e., the possibility to cast a vote) and the "passive" right (i.e., the possibility of running in an election). (translator's note)

running farms and businesses, women, at least in big cities and especially in the north, came out of the millenary social exile that had seen them shut in their homes overseeing domestic life and bringing up children. The end of the war would not shut them up again.

One of the unresolved questions left by the conflict was precisely the reinstatement of women in a context in which—once the emergency was over—the demands made by feminist movements were viewed with annoyance. The Fascist movement, born of the mayhem of the postwar years, certainly had its own vision of the role women were to play, but was also aware of the increased social and political weight of their representation. This vision evolved in the course of time and, de facto, triggered specific legislation. But what the effects of the regime's choices were and what they were driven by is a complex matter.

The Ninth Congress of the Pro-suffrage International Federation, the international organization that fought for the extension to women of the right to vote, opened in Italy on May 14, 1923. Attending the event, Mussolini, who had only been in office for a few months, made an extremely binding programmatic speech in which, "he solemnly promised the vote for Italian women, saying that he felt 'authorized to declare that, barring unforeseeable events, the Fascist government pledged to grant the vote to several categories of women, starting from the administrative field'."[2] It was a solemn pledge and it bound the regime to pursue a policy of emancipation.

It has to be admitted that the promise—or at least its premises—was effectively kept as the regime granted women the right to vote in local elections on November 22, 1925.[3] But what appeared to be a fundamental conquest turned out to be an utter farce. First of all, it needs to be underlined that suffrage granted was not universal. In order to vote, women had to be over twenty-five years of age and possess specific characteristics: eligible, for example, were the mothers and wives of soldiers who had fallen for the fatherland, women with medals, women with parental authority, women who could read and write, women with elementary school-leaving certificates and women who paid local income taxes of over a hundred lire a year. These restrictions considerably reduced the number of female voters and reserved a right promised to all women only to a minority of well-off, educated women.

"He was the first to really think about women!"

The law was published in the *Gazzetta Ufficiale*, or Official Gazette, the official journal of records of the Italian goverment, on December 9, 1925. At the same time, however, an electoral reform was already being debated in parliament that was far more robust and, potentially, would have much more of an impact on the daily lives of Italians. On February 4, 1926, in fact, the reform of the administrative arrangement of communes and provinces was introduced.[4] This measure abolished elected posts at local administrative level en bloc, centralizing appointments and placing them in the hands of the national executive. The law providing for the vote to some women, published only two months earlier, no longer made sense, for no women had had the chance to assert their right. In this case, nonetheless, the Fascists did establish a system of equality of sorts since the right to vote at local elections was taken away from men too.

Women's suffrage was only really granted in Italy in February 1945, when the government of national unity presided over by Ivanoe Bonomi guaranteed it to all women over twenty-one (excluding prostitutes who worked outside licensed brothels).[5] Women voted for the first time in some local elections. The following year, in March 1946, they were allowed access to the "passive" vote, meaning that they could run for election too.[6] On June 2, 1946, all Italian women were called to vote for the election of the Constituent Assembly and the referendum for the choice between monarchy and republic.

The vote for women was thus one of the many promises that the Fascist regime failed to keep.

Voting aside

More generally speaking, the relationship between the regime and women was, at best, ambiguous. On the one hand, propaganda placed Mussolini's dream of the "new Italian man" alongside that of the "new Italian woman," the other half of the regime's social anthropology project. On the other, the Fascists followed the paternalistic, male chauvinist line firmly rooted in society and, in the course of time, systematically circumscribed the public space available to women and limited their autonomy.

Once he had consolidated his power, the *Duce* set about putting his theory of the greatness and progress of Italian society into practice with a plan in which women had a very clear role. In the Fascist revolution, women were expected, above all, to give birth to new Italians, preferably male, to turn into soldiers. The marginalization of women socially was accompanied by another of the regime's desires, namely the quantitative and qualitative growth of the Italian people. Women were not to waste time in the affairs of men and were only expected to produce children. The attentions dedicated by the regime to women and the family context as a whole were instruments, designed to make the woman not a social subject but an object of the policy of totalitarian power. By virtue of their role as procreators of new young Italians (read Fascists), women came to be seen essentially as "female breeders," thereby consolidating an already firmly established stereotype of Italian society. All the concrete actions implemented by the regime in this field were based on the premise that women were "wombs," not individuals.

The first Fascist organic law of note, for example, was the one establishing the National Agency for the Protection of Mothers and Children (Opera Nazionale per la Protezione della Maternità e dell'Infanzia).[7] The institution, which centralized and harmonized already existing public measures in the field of help for women and minors, focused not on the protection of women as individuals but, rather, on the act of giving birth to children. Article 4 of the law made clear that, "The Opera Nazionale provides, both directly and through its provincial and communal branches, for the protection of expectant mothers and needy or abandoned mothers."[8] The qualification was made not by gender but by function: "expectant mothers" and "needy or abandoned mothers" as opposed to women. The same principle underpinned legislation on the maternity of workers,[9] which, among other things, excluded housewives and home workers who constituted the majority of the female work force at the time.

This was, in practice, the Fascist imagination's prevailing vision of women, not altogether different from the one that the patriarchal Catholic tradition had already etched in Italian society. In this way, the Fascists tended to relegate women to a subordinate social role. A specific characteristic of Fascism was, however, to keep in check and neutralize the nascent women's rights movement in Italy. Although in 1928 the National Federation for Women's Suffrage and Civil and Political Rights (Federazione Nazionale per il Suffragio e i Diritti Civili e Politici della Donna) was still reminding Mussolini of his unkept promises in an open letter,[10] by the 1930s the federation was already silent and inert. The general restriction of the civil liberties of Italians left no room at all for specific gender grievances.

Not only were there laws intended to protect procreation, a whole set of measures also strived to restrict the freedom of action of women as citizens. One of the greatest difficulties in implementing the Fascists' plan to reduce women to mere "incubators" was forcing them to stay home. The fundamental legislative action used to do this was the modification of labour law to exclude women from the workforce. The possibility for women to earn a wage of their own and be independent was in fact the main obstacle to the construction of the domestic cage into which they were to be shut.

To develop this maneuver aimed at destroying women's aspirations, the Fascists worked on two fronts: the economic one, where it progressively expelled women from the workforce, hence depriving them of their economic independence; and the cultural one, where it excluded them from the education system, both as teachers and as students and as administrative workers.

Private charter schools, like those run by religious institutions and foreign schools in Italy, were the first to be affected. Article 50 of Royal Decree no. 1084 of June 1925[11] established that in these institutions "women cannot take part in competitions for managerial posts."[12]

Just a year later, in 1926, women were prevented from teaching science subjects in technical colleges and literature and philosophy in high schools.[13] This legislation was doubly discriminatory since it deprived women of the possibility of teaching subjects, such as literature and philosophy, at high schools with an emphasis on the humanities, which were to become central under Giovanni Gentile's subsequent Fascist education reform. It made clear that women, excluded as they were from teaching the subjects that characterized syllabuses, would never be able to be class teachers. It also took away the possibility for women to have socially prestigious, well-paid careers, while at the same time emphasizing that certain subjects, such as the theoretical ones, were outside their reach. It has to be said, however, that one position was reserved exclusively to women, that of "gardening mistress," gardening being an optional subject in teacher training schools.

Public sector employment was traditionally a very desirable one for women, but was also the one it was easiest to control through legislation. The public sector began to be seen as a place from which to expel women, making room for men and reducing the range of possibilities for getting away from home.

In 1933, the Fascists agreed to the organization of competitions for jobs in the public administrations from which women could be excluded.[14] With this discriminatory measure, which envisaged limitations solely and exclusively to the number of women (the possibility of holding public competitions without the participation of men was obviously not provided for) public entities were prevented from establishing workplaces to which women were allowed truly equal access. It was thus possible to masculinize the state apparatus, local level included, without hindrance.

In 1934 the presence of women in local government was limited.[15] The underlying belief was that they were unsuitable for government and public administration work. A close look at the evolution of the Fascists' misogynous legislation, however, shows that women did not accept this type of exclusion lying down, and in 1938 a special law had to be passed to limit the percentage of women employed in public offices and private enterprises to no more than 10 per cent of the total workforce.[16] In the case of enterprises and entities with fewer than ten employees, such as small communal administrations and companies, excluding family businesses, it was expressly forbidden to employ female personnel. This particularly rigid law, which was hard to enforce, envisaged the firing of thousands of skilled female office and factory workers and secretaries, and blocked access to the workforce for young women who were studying for a career in industry and the public and private services.

This veritable lockout had many consequences. One effect of the regime's labor and family policies was, for example, the loss of social value of the training and education young women had acquired. Studying subjects that had nothing to do with home economics and management became superfluous. The "new Italian women" were expected to be well-mannered as opposed to well-educated.

These obviously misogynous measures demonstrate, how the Fascists, in their popular rhetoric, felt that women were inferior, unsuited for governmental and administrative responsibilities.

Women were progressively and systematically removed from active life and the workforce in a masculinization of society that went hand in hand with the brutalization of public discourse. The Fascist ideal was young, strong and, above all, male. The Fascist vision of woman was that of a mother, a wife and, if the worst came to the worst, a widow. Her place was in the home, where she had to be shut up to tend solely to domestic chores and children.

In addition to laws that sought to exclude women from public life, other legislation forced them into a subordinate role in domestic life too. Article 587 of the new Penal Code, introduced in 1930, provided for the infamous extenuating circumstances for so-called crimes of honor: "Anyone who causes the death of their wife, daughter or sister in the act of discovering their unlawful relations and in a fit of fury at the resultant offense to his or his family's honor is punished with a prison sentence of three to seven years."[17]

This clause, which was repealed from the Italian legal system only in 1981, established two fundamental principles: the concept that honor was a strictly male characteristic and that the boundaries of its lawful defense extended to a man's closest relatives. A "dishonored" woman was also dishonoring the man closest to her, but he could wash this dishonor away with blood, confident of the clemency of the institutions.

The second principle is that the life of a woman was in fact worth less than that of a man. In a period in which the institution of divorce did not exist, the extenuating circumstances guaranteed by the article were a constant threat to women in search of independence, to women who wanted to build themselves autonomous life paths, maybe with another man. The article was an implicit endorsement of femicide.

Article 544, which formalized so-called "forced weddings," had the same tone. Anyone committing sexual violence against a woman (minors included) would have his crime discharged if he married her. In addition to the obvious barbarity of condemning a woman to live with her molester for the rest of her life, the article established that the woman's will was totally superfluous in a marriage. The definitions of the crimes of rape and incest, which were reduced to acts against morality, not against the individual, followed the same line. This article of the Penal Code too was only abrogated in 1981.[18]

For Fascism, this attack on women's independence and equality with men was not occasional but systematic. Mention should also be made of a particular aspect typical of public discourse at the time, which was tied to the concept of fertility but also spilled over into unbridled sexual behaviour. Stories abound—in part true, in part not—about Mussolini's sexual freedom and voracity. He was open about and even flaunted his infidelities, which the regime itself used to fuel the myth of the "masculine" *Duce*.

The image of the leader's "woman" was two-fold. On the one hand was the domestic hand-maid vividly represented by Rachele Guidi, who Fascist propaganda, sure enough, dubbed "Donna Rachele": the *Duce*'s wife who gave him five children, took care of the family and, apparently indifferent to his blatant betrayals, ensured her husband unconditional fidelity.[19] On the other hand were his lovers, some with illegitimate children. The last one, whose role was almost that of his official favourite, was Clara Petacci, the sexual object, popularly known by the diminutive "Claretta," as if she were a child, ever a minor in the eyes of the *Duce* and public opinion. A fine trophy for a man approaching old age. As faithful to the *Duce* as his wife, she shared the same violent end and posthumous public profanation as Mussolini. The tragic exhibition of her corpse alongside that of the dictator was the final image of the Fascist woman.

"Plus, he was handsome! Everybody loved him!"

CHAPTER 7

Mussolini the Condottiere and Statesman

Was the *Duce* a great leader?

Even though Fascist militarism performed feebly in virtually all the theatres of war, there are still latter-day fans of the regime who argue that the Fascist war machine was not as awful as the disasters in Africa, Asia and Western and Eastern Europe might lead to suspect. With one of the largest naval forces in the world and an air force that piled up one record after another before the war, the *Duce*'s weaponry, claim online haters, could not have been all that bad and, in any case, the fault was not his but that of his henchmen, who were incapable of running the war.

"He made Italy great and respected by all!"

Many ways could be found to establish whether Mussolini possessed the qualities of a military leader. Over the years, regime propaganda built a solid myth based mainly on uniforms and theatrical parades, which cast the figure of the *Duce* in stone as the military as well as political leader of the Fascist system. The term *Duce* itself derives from the Latin *dux*, an honorary title reserved in ancient Rome to victorious commanders and great civil administrators. In order to understand what the term *"grande condottiero"* meant, it may be useful to contextualise the relationship between Mussolini and the military.

The young Benito took his first stand on the matter at the age of nineteen when he emigrated to Switzerland and dodged compulsory military service in the Royal Army.[1] Then a socialist agitator, he professed to be anything but a warmonger, and avoided rendering to his country a service that he was to regard as sacred when he took power. This initially sincere antipathy to militarism was offset in part when, for reasons of expediency, he decided to volunteer for the Great War, a symbolic, unsolicited gesture that landed him in the trenches.

After rising to the rank of corporal major, he attended an officer training course but failed to qualify. He was also wounded—in an accidental mortar explosion,[2] not in combat—but this was enough to earn him discharge and the right to the title of war veteran. The experience proved very useful for him in the post-war environment, where he acquired prestige in the veteran and shock troop circles that were to form the base for *squadrismo*, the Fascist action squads. This sweeping evolution, almost a volte-face from his early socialist ideas, testifies to the complexity of the relationship between the future *Duce* and military matters.

The attention of the social media users who sing the praises of Fascism's military achievements focuses on the presumed victories of the regime's war machine, which, they argue, marked a period of glory for the Italian armed forces. The culpably disastrous handling of World War II was not enough to diminish Fascism's aura as a capable and well-organized military movement. For twenty years, the aim of the regime was to shape the Italian people according to the principles of force and warlike virility, and the practices of indoctrination and rhetoric left a deep furrow in people's imaginations about the period. To this day, it is difficult to imagine Fascism without all its paraphernalia of weaponry and uniforms and goose-stepping. To understand how much this military spirit was sincere and how much it was affected, and how much the responsibility for this image should be ascribed to Mussolini the *condottiere* and not to the propaganda machine, it might be useful to scan some episodes from the Fascists' military adventures.

The first acid test for this thirst for power was Libya: the Italian colony, seized from the Ottoman Empire in 1911 under one of the many Giolitti governments, was still a territory ready for "pacification" in the early 1920s. Only the narrow coastal strip and principal ports were in Italian hands, while the interior was still controlled by Arab and Berber populations. In this case too, the opportunity offered to Fascist propaganda was extremely tempting. As soon as it had taken power, the regime decided to make Libya the symbol of the birth of a new way of interpreting the government's role in shaping the bodies and minds of citizens: "For Mussolini, the 'new Italian' meant above all a new soldier, more tenacious, more aggressive, and even more cruel, who worthily befitted the myth of the Roman spirit and made people forget the mediocre or dire showings of "Italietta"* over the years."[3]

It was thus that the Fascists, adopting a new way of waging war, aggressive and ferocious, embarked on the so-called reconquest of Libya. Wave after wave, Italian soldiers advanced into the desert inland from the coastal cities in an effort to impose the supremacy of Fascist weapons. The struggle was evidently uneven: machine-guns,

---

* Literally "Little Italy," the derogatory term used by the Fascists to refer to the part of society that opposed the regime and championed pacifism and parliamentary democracy. (translator's note)

airplanes and motor vehicles against bands of desert guerrillas armed with makeshift weapons, mostly old rifles. The regime's propaganda did not miss the opportunity to glamorize what was, to all intents and purposes, the attempted genocide of the desert populations with a romantic sense of exotic conquest.

The effects on the population of this military campaign are addressed in Chapter 8. Here it is enough to note how the war on bands of isolated and disorganized guerrillas dragged on for almost ten years and was declared over only in 1931—and only at the cost of violence on and abuse of the civilian population. Far from being an example of Italian efficiency and fighting ability, it was a demonstration of how ill-advised and poorly thought-out the country's colonial policy actually was at the time. Among other things, as far as the control of the territory was concerned, pacification and normalization failed to meld, and many zones stayed essentially under military occupation for the duration of the colonial period.

The pacification of Somalia—a territory the Italians had controlled since the late nineteenth century—played out in an even more singular fashion. The colony, which had never created particular problems and lived in a climate in which the interests of Italian agricultural concession holders and the drive for autonomy of local sultanates balanced off, was laid to waste during the five-year term of office of the quadrumvir Cesare de Vecchi.[*][4] This Turinese Fascist Party boss waged a sort of *squadrista*-style guerrilla war, which proved expensive for the state coffers and alienated the resident population, its sole purpose being to earn him fame as a *condottiere*. Individualism and haphazardness characterized all Fascist military adventures.

When, in 1935, the Fascists decided to embark on what, propaganda-wise, was to be its most important venture, that is to say the conquest of Ethiopia, it deployed an incredibly large amount of resources. Huge investments were made to enhance their image and the aim was "a great and immediate demonstration of prestige."[5] The Fascist leaders were well aware of the risks involved if they failed to achieve their objective, namely the conquest of an empire, Ethiopia, which had been painted as a sort of barbaric relic opposed to the reborn civilization of Rome. About 330,000 troops were sent to fight in Ethiopia in 1935, a figure that increased to

---

[*]   Cesare De Vecchi (1884-1959) was a Fascist politician and colonial governor, first of Italian Somaliland, then of the Aegean Islands. He was one of the four *quadrumviri* (modelled on the ancient Roman quadrumvirs), the four "strong men" chosen by Mussolini to lead his March on Rome in October 1922. The others were Michele Bianchi, Emilio De Bono and Italo Balbo. (translator's note)

560,000 during the course of the war, and three billion tons of arms and materiel were delivered to the field.[6] The state coffers were drained to supply the troops with every military technology available, including chemical weapons such as mustard gas and arsine.[7]

Many *gerarchi*, Fascist Party bosses, set out on an adventure that appeared to hold the promise of easy glory: even the *Duce*'s own sons, Bruno and Vittorio Mussolini, and his son-in-law, Galeazzo Ciano, joined the war. All three took part in the campaign in air force bombers, a safer way than others to wage war against a country totally devoid of aircraft and anti-aircraft artillery.[8] In the course of the seven-month military campaign, the rules of the Geneva Convention regarding civilians and prisoners of war were systematically broken and the theory of terror was applied against the local populations. Moreover, to prevent international organizations from sending aid to the Ethiopians or giving evidence of Italian atrocities, the Red Cross was bombed for the first time in history.[9]

The hurry to proclaim victory meant that the campaign was declared accomplished with the conquest of the Ethiopian capital Addis Ababa, even though a large portion of the national territory was still outside Italian control. In reality, the empire of the Negus was never totally subdued and Italian authority did not go beyond where Italian weaponry was installed.[10] This was the beginning of a fierce and costly occupation that assumed the connotations of guerrilla warfare with the arrival of Marshal Rodolfo Graziani, who applied terror to "pacify" the local populations.

Graziani was the most conspicuous product of the Fascist military apparatus: a senior official at the time of the March on Rome, he was quick to swear allegiance to Fascism when it became clear that the Fascists were about to conquer power.[11] He stood out not only for his cruelty but also for a certain ability in extricating himself from political squabbling and hanging on to power. He was the main culprit for the massacres committed by Italians in the colonies in the 1930s. He joined the Salò Republic (RSI or Repubblica Sociale Italiana)* in 1943, and Libya and Ethiopia demanded his extradition as a war criminal, but in vain, at the end of the war.

As far as Italy's other military adventure in the 1930s, the Spanish Civil War, is concerned, what was supposed to have been external support for the coup-leader General Franco soon became a

---

* The Salò Republic, or Repubblica Sociale Italiana (RSI) was the name given to the rump of Italy left in Nazi-Fascist hands and governed by Mussolini following German occupation in September 1943. Salò is the small town on Lake Garda where most of the Republic's ministries were situated. (translator's note)

full-fledged military intervention. At first, voluntary contingents of Blackshirts were supplemented by "forced volunteer" soldiers, organized into formations that were nominally independent but actually led by officers in the Royal Army.[12] When the effort went on for longer than the regime had anticipated, Mussolini was forced to deploy regular troops to avoid losing face, thus initiating a full-blown campaign alongside the participants in the Spanish military coup.

In this case too, Fascist troops found themselves pitched against opponents who were poorer armed with fewer supplies, but still there was no lack of defeats in the field. One that had a significant effect on the morale of the Fascist troops was that at Guadalajara, on March 8, 1937, where four fully-armed divisions of the finest 40,000 men the regime could marshal were badly beaten by the Republicans. The humiliating defeat was exacerbated by the fact that the Italian Fascists were stopped by the Battaglione Garibaldi, made up of Italian anti-Fascists who had gone to Spain to defend the Republic. As Angelo Del Boca points out, it was a severe blow for Mussolini: "Not only had the 'new Italians' forged by the regime been resoundingly defeated, they had been defeated by other Italians who had not attended Fascist Saturdays."[13]

Better fortunes awaited the air force which, having destroyed its weak Republican counterpart with German help, began applying the terrorist techniques tried and tested in Libya, Somalia and Ethiopia. Republican towns and cities were bombed with the precise aim of sowing panic behind the anti-Fascist lines, neglecting military targets to concentrate on civilian ones. The most glaring example, for number of dead and international outrage was the three-day raid ordered directly by Mussolini on Barcelona from March 16 to 18, 1938, which according to reports caused from six hundred to one thousand three hundred civilian victims.[14] The Fascist air force also took part in the sadly famous bombing of Guernica, which killed more than two hundred of the small Basque town's inhabitants and inspired Pablo Picasso's masterpiece.

Like all the regime's enterprises, Spain was marketed as a prestige victory, even though it opened a gaping hole in the state budget and was a stain on what passed for the "honor of the Italian armed forces."

Things did not go much better when the European situation came to a head. While Mussolini's overbearing ally, Nazi Germany, reaped international successes and annexed new territories, for Fascist Italy, with its economy crippled and its exhausted armed forces scattered across a number of different theaters of war, even the foray with which it occupied Albania (April 7-12, 1939) proved complex, though the country was already virtually an Italian protectorate in which a segment of the establishment intended to support annexation.

When World War II broke out, the state of exhaustion of the armed forces was such that Mussolini reluctantly had to refuse to enter the war immediately at Germany's side. Following the Wehrmacht's invasion of Poland, the *Duce* was forced to proclaim a cosmetic neutrality, defined with an ad hoc neologism as one of "non-belligerence." In practice, the regime that had claimed for twenty years that it was anxiously awaiting a decisive clash of civilizations between the new Fascist ideology and the old liberal democracies had to admit, when the fateful moment arrived, that it was not ready.

Too many organizational aspects had been overlooked, too many wrong decisions made. The navy, for example, which absorbed a hefty portion of the Fascist military budget, focused by the *Duce*'s express will on the building of enormous battleships. These prestigious vessels with prodigious firepower were an excellent propaganda symbol of military and technological strength. Even though the widespread conviction at the time was that naval battles would increasingly be decided by the deployment of airplanes, the Italian navy obeyed the *Duce*'s will and remained faithful to nineteenth-century naval theories. Whereas other countries with great military fleets were building aircraft carriers, Italy spent huge sums of money on obsolete ships which, among other things, consumed too much fuel for a nation with no oil, and were too precious to be "wasted." The result was they were effectively used by Italian navy for only one task throughout the Second World War: namely, trying to make sure that supplies reached Libya safely.

The military apparatus was exhausted but also badly led. Twenty years of political cronyism, in which individuals whose sole merit was blind loyalty were put in positions of power, meant that key positions were occupied by people who were incompetent or, at best, inexperienced. Even armaments were obsolete and of the poorest quality as a result of widespread corruption in the military procurement business.[15]

It was Hitler's hurry to act that brought everything to a head and it was only Mussolini's altogether embarrassing reading of the international geopolitical situation that drove him to line up a country that he knew to be unprepared with another that at that moment appeared to be winning. His behavior was not only disgraceful, it was also counterproductive. From Italy's declaration of war against France and England on June 10, 1940, onwards, Italy continued in vain to pursue prestige and to attempt to repair increasingly bitter humiliations.[16] The very brief campaign in France against an enemy that had already been defeated provided immediate evidence of the lack of preparation and incompetence of the Italian command. Just a few days into the war, the Italians, unable to break through the front, recorded 1,258 dead, the French just twenty.[17]

An emblematic example of *"condottiero"* Mussolini's way of conceiving the conflict was his attempt to pursue a "parallel war" to that of the Germans with the opening of the Balkan front. The attack on Greece (October 28, 1940–April 23, 1941) was a consequence of the regime's will to impose its own military initiative and display offensive capabilities autonomous from those of its German allies. The mission was a total fiasco which, to all intents and purposes, put an end to any Italian claims to carry on the war without the Germans. Hurried and poorly organized, without any purpose other than to accumulate victories on the field, the Greek campaign demonstrated how unreliable the Fascists' claims about Italy's military strength were.

The regime had already been given a hard time during missions that on paper ought to have been easier to complete, such as those in Ethiopia against what was considered to be a primitive army, and against the Republican forces in Spain, often made up of volunteers. When it came to fighting a regular army, albeit of limited importance, like that of Greece, the Fascist offensive was humiliated: the chain of command was inadequate, the mid-level cadres were confused, and the soldiers were demotivated and very poorly equipped. Twenty years of Fascism had not created a new warrior spirit in Italians after all and, when push came to shove, they failed to live up to a military tradition that, for better or for worse, had been victorious in the Great War.

The handling of the war also involved a string of paradoxical blunders verging on naivety: for example, after years spent hanging Berbers and Arabs to overcome their resistance, at the height of the conflict Mussolini tried to call Muslims to a holy war against the British in North Africa, receiving by way of response only sarcasm and ambushes along the caravan routes.

Even strategic decisions were botched: insisting on fighting a war against the Soviets with an entire army corps—even if the German high command had declined the offer of an Italian expeditionary force—was a glaring example of this. The Italian attack force for the Russian campaign was withdrawn from much closer battlefronts[18] and sent to certain defeat without adequate materiel.[19] What was intended to be the "glorious anti-Bolshevik crusade" was a shameful massacre.

The *Duce* is to be considered one of the chief culprits for the disaster. He was guilty not only of negligence in military procurement and bad appointments of inept military commanders. Mussolini also declared on more than one occasion that he was counting on an anthropological revolution that would transform the Italian people into a people of warriors and conquerors. It was per se somewhat humiliating for a society to be seen solely as a mass in need of being shaped, and the concept ultimately did not work. Italians failed to grasp the point of the Fascist war, if there was one, and the *Duce* often complained angrily about the fact.

When failures became evident and impossible to conceal, the leader of the regime reacted by calling Italians a people of weaklings, unworthy of the destiny he had planned for them. In view of the way in which Mussolini had "prepared the future" for his people, his was an ungenerous conclusion and, above all, he absolved himself of all responsibility.

"Mussolini saved Italy from destruction. If Italy emerged from the Second World War unscathed and without dramatic consequences, it owes it to him. He loved his people right to the last."

Signed, apparently, Albert Einstein

If the historical duty of the *condottiere*, of the *Duce*, was to lead his people into war by preparing them for the challenges ahead and for greatness, Mussolini and Fascism did none of this, despite the Fascist hyperbole still to be heard that underpins a certain nostalgic narrative of the times in which "Italy was respected." The Italy that fought World War II had a social fabric worn out by expansionist policies that had brought no tangible advantages and an economic and military apparatus unprepared for the conflict, already exhausted by too many rash adventures. Above all, it failed to grasp the reasons why it had entered war in the first place.

The notably sudden dissolution of a twenty-year regime in the summer of 1943 may also be explained by great disillusion with a flimsy narrative that had held up for a generation only because not enough people had had the courage to say that the emperor, or rather the *Duce*, had no clothes.

CHAPTER 8

Mussolini the Humanitarian

Was the *Duce* a "benign" dictator?

One of the chief errors in perception of the Fascist regime and Mussolini himself is that Fascism was a totalitarianism "with a human face."

This is a particularly hard claim to analyze since it involves taking a set of very different points into account. Most justifications flounder on the fact that Fascism spared no efforts in consciously compressing the civil liberties of Italians. The freedom of thought and expression, association and movement were all systematically persecuted. These deprivations were justified by the need to consolidate the new state structure, but the freedoms were abolished once and for all when the Mussolini government had been ruling for ten years. Yet either out of conviction or simply to be argumentative, some people believe that this type of limitation is not enough to condemn the twenty years of Fascist rule.

In assessments of this period of Italian history, the Fascist regime is often compared with contemporaneous totalitarian regimes. Mussolini would appear to have been a much nicer man than Hitler, for example. There are many reasons for this consolidated view, not only among revisionists but also in Italian society in general. Still today very few people are prepared to liken twenty years of Fascism to ten years of Nazi terror. This phenomenon of self-absolution is typically Italian and was caused by a lack of postwar reflection about what Fascism had really been. The "Italians are nice people" myth was perpetuated and still dies hard today, while the Italian partisan resistance movement from 1943 to 1945 was enough to wipe from the memory of Italians the fact that for twenty years the Fascist regime had enjoyed the approval of the majority of the population.

The Allies forced post-war Germany to come to terms with Nazism: one way of doing this was by proposing convenient narrative solutions and allowing the great deceit perpetrated—and the spell cast—by the Führer to overshadow mass consensus. The process of "de-Nazification" was instituted and pursued by the Allies, and though in many cases the results were disappointing, the debate on the responsibility of German society had begun and is still underway.

An analogous process of "de-Fascistization" has never taken place in Italy. Accepting that two whole decades in the country's life had been a major historical blunder that had wrought grief and destruction was too much for a generation of individuals who, though born and bred under Fascism, felt the need to turn a new page after the tragedies of war and rebuild from scratch not only a nation but also their sense of belonging to a community.

The convenient choice was thus taken to put the blame for the majority of the horrors of the conflict and the causes that sparked it on the German allies and Nazism. For many, the comparison between Fascism and National Socialism made the first look like a sort of watered-down version of the second. At most, certain behaviors of the Italian dictatorship were passed off—and still are—as caricatural, almost comical. The very term "Nazi-Fascism," coined to describe Mussolini's regime from 1943 to 1945 and identifying the Fascism of the Salò Republic and Nazism as a single concept, is open to an interpretation that is undeclared but very tempting. If, in fact, after 1943 it was necessary to find a new term to define late-Fascism—the Fascism of the massacres of Italians and deportations—the semantic choice obviously presupposed that before this "evil Fascism" there had been a less bloody, hence "benign Fascism" in Italy. This narrative, which has been edulcorated in the course of time— partly by the twilight of the republican rhetoric of a modern Italy "reborn" with the Resistance and anti-Fascism—has gained increasing ground to the point that the language of politics has dismissed Fascist violence as "a holiday."[1]

Today no real condemnation of Italian Fascism seems forthcoming; indeed, even public demonstrations of Fascist revisionism are dismissed, even by law, as acts of "commemoration."[2]

This moral leniency has spawned more than one legend and set many a self-absolution mechanism into motion. It may therefore be useful to make a detailed examination of Mussolini and Fascism's modus operandi to better appreciate to what extent the first totalitarianism of the twentieth century can be considered "benign."

"Mussolini is the only politician to have loved his people!"

Was Mussolini a racist?

Among the many legends eddying about on how Fascism was benign, one in particular serves to stave off the accusation of racism: it claims that the dictatorship was not racist at all and that the 1938 racial laws were merely a yielding to the will of its German ally. In other words, the body of laws was imposed by Hitler while the Fascist government only applied them very blandly. Over the years, one part of the revisionist discourse has argued that the *Duce* actually helped Jews escape from the clutches of Nazism. In order to refute this interpretation and set the relationship between Fascists and Nazis into context, it is necessary to return to the cultural environment in which Fascism was born and developed.

Italian racism before Mussolini

It is necessary, first of all, to remember that the world that gave life to Fascism was genuinely racist too, at least insofar as all the societies that supported or failed to boycott the colonialism of their own states were racist. Countries with colonialist policies developed—consciously or even only as a corollary to their own geopolitical action—a mentality of racial dominance to legitimize themselves.

The concept of innate or natural differences between the various peoples of the world had been established by the Italian legal system long before 1922: the legislation that structured the judicial administration of the colonies was blatantly discriminatory towards so-called Indigenous peoples, in the case of Italy as in that of other European powers. The Royal Decree of 1902[3] which framed the Eritrean judicial system, for example, envisaged that local courts of justice would have no jurisdiction over Italian colonials and that, in the event of disputes between Italians or those "assimilated" and the colonized people, the judge had to be Italian.

The wording "assimilated" was especially telling since it essentially comprised all white Europeans present on the colonial territory. This firmly-rooted western racism was closely linked to Kipling's concept of "the white man's burden":[4] irrespective of their provenance, the whites in the colony constituted a single community, which shared the privileges and duties arising from their being a "superior race." Two different legislations were necessary because, after all, the natives could not be expected to observe the laws codified for the Europeans. As the historian Luciano Martone baldly points out, "the savage—or so the supporters of the special code believed—commits crimes driven by motives that belong to the orbit of ethnic beliefs, fanatisms and prejudices inherited from his social complex."[5] This was the belief not only of the legislators but also of most of Italian society at the time.

It is pointless to discuss the underlying racism of the Fascists in the 1920s because it was a conception quite evenly spread over all the social strata of Italy in those days. If anything, what may differentiate popular racism from specifically Fascist racism is the building of the myth of the Italian race. This mania of Mussolini's appears to have resulted from his reading of a mixture of classical and modern texts. He spoke publicly of the "Latin race" as opposed to the Anglo-Saxon long before the foundation of the Fascist movement. In a speech in Bologna on May 19, 1918, when he was still only one of the many seeking to turn the ferment of ideas created by a war that was still in progress into a political narrative, he cited H. G. Wells who, speaking of the characteristic features of the Latin race, wrote that, "they feel the beauty of personal audacity, the fascination of risk and they have the taste for adventure."[6] To Mussolini the simple political agitator, the traits that defined the concepts of race applied to geopolitics were already visible. These characteristics were predefined by genetics and, in part, by climate, which implied predestination in one's way of living in the world and fighting.

That race and races are a central theme in Mussolini's thought transpires from his never casual use of the term. As the historian Emilio Gentile points out, "Mussolini believed that 'race is a fact as hard as granite,' as he wrote on February 1, 1921, and this fact rendered internationalism 'an absurd fairy tale,' because the deep masses do not and cannot override—and this is a great fortune—the irrepressible fact of race and nation."[7]

In his first speech to the Chamber of Deputies on June 21, 1921, Mussolini defined the newly acquired Italian province of Alto Adige as "a multilingual region where the contrast between races is ancient and very sharp."[8] The subject of racial difference was once again the pivot of his thinking about a territory and how to inhabit it. In this case too, the different, hence incompatible, races were once again the Latin and the "Nordic."

In the course of time, the future *Duce*'s rhetoric about the problem of race became more polished, more contextualized, enhanced by new elements. He supplemented his pseudo-scientific approach with the experience of hatred for the enemy incarnated in war propaganda. This hatred for an "other," who had to be not only defeated but annihilated, was the result of long years of trench warfare against an invisible enemy who had to be destroyed with bombs, machine guns and gas. The inability to understand the other, which turned into a will to exterminate, ran in parallel with the elevation of the main object of the warlike rhetoric of the time—the *patria*, or motherland—to a veritable religion.

It was the trenches that saw the birth of what Emilio Gentile calls "the myth of Italy, that is to say faith in a new primacy for Italy, the fusion between right-wing radicalism and left-wing radicalism, preparing the ground for the new synthesis of Fascism."[9] It was from the trenches too that Fascism borrowed the idea of being the only phenomenon capable of physically representing this "Italianism," and that anyone opposed to it was anthropologically different: "In fact, political adversaries were seen by Fascism as anthropologically incompatible with the new Italy that had arisen from the war. Anti-Fascists were humanly despicable, violent out of cowardice, greedy only for material goods; they disowned the *patria* and for this very reason were no longer Italians but, rather, anti-Italians deserving of persecution and elimination."[10]

Hate was at the center of the thinking of what might be called the "Fascism of the streets," namely the Fascism fuelled by the street violence of the first post-World War I years, in which hardcore *squadrismo* cleaved to elements of fear of diversity typical of the military context of the conflict. Fascism originally called for the death of its foes, such as socialists, "insofar as they are socialists," irretrievably different people, hence deserving of being destroyed. *Squadristi* did not disdain to shoot and throw bombs at workers' marches, even if women and children were present[11]—because they saw the red scum as a formless mass of enemies. These were harsh words, altogether identical to the ones that Hitler reserved for the Jews in the same period.

This underlying violence, which was not an extreme tool used in struggle but the very essence of the politics of Fascism as a movement, made the street clashes of 1921 and 1922 particularly violent. Gaetano Salvemini records that about three thousand people were killed by the *squadristi* in those two years alone.[12] Fascism grew as a movement by immediately distinguishing who was worthy of being Italian from who was not: once the Fascists had taken power, they shifted their sights from socialists to liberals to the progressive middle classes. For the first time in history, a government theorized the enemies of the state and spared no efforts in eradicating them.

From its infancy, Fascist rhetoric declared that the movement's secular mission was to construct a "new man." Emilio Gentile observes that, "Mussolini and the Fascists saw themselves as a vanguard of new Italians whose ambition was to conduct an anthropological revolution to forge a new Italian race of dominators, conquerors and creators of civilization."[13]

In power against others

Just as Nazism condensed its own violent racism in Staatsfeinde's definition "enemies of the state," of whom Jews were the predominant component (supplemented by communists, homosexuals, Jehovah's witnesses, social outcasts and so on), so the Fascist rhetoric of Mussolini constructed, first and foremost, an effective "rhetoric of the enemy" against all opponents and "deviants." The first victims of violence were people with different political beliefs, but soon the Fascists were targeting social differences and, once in power, ethnic differences too.

The indiscriminate massacres perpetrated to "pacify" the colony in Libya were the first example of how the Fascists intended to deal with anybody who did not bow to the rhetoric of the *patria*. The use of gas against civilians, terrorist bombing and decimations were all crimes committed according to the racist logic whereby a whole people was guilty of given misdeeds by birth. The man called in to head the repression, or "reconquest" as it was known, was Rodolfo Graziani, who during his time on Libya had significantly earned himself the nickname of "butcher of the Arabs."[14]

The work of "pacification" was carried on with every means: one of the most brutal was the deportation of whole populations from the interior to concentration camps on the coast in order to deprive Libyan fighters of the local assistance they could normally rely on. War was waged on the Berbers as a people, without distinguishing either between civilians and partisan fighters or between those fit for military service and others: deportations and massacres involved women, children and the elderly, without distinction. The rules of engagement that were later to be applied in the Fascist massacres in Central and Northern

Italy during the War of Liberation were already effective and active at the end of the 1920s. In Libya it was Graziani himself who issued the crime figures: no fewer than a hundred thousand people were imprisoned in the concentration camps installed near Italian strongholds,[15] but after the camps were dismantled in 1933 fewer than sixty thousand were able to return to their homes.[16]

For Giorgio Rochat, "the deportation of the peoples of the Gebel and their subsequent slaughter constitute perhaps the most serious crime of Italian colonialism."[17] According to Italian census figures, if the population of Libya in 1921 numbered around 570,000, in 1931, it had dropped to 512,000. With deportations, mass killings and forced migrations, 58,000 people or 10 per cent of the population had thus gone missing.

This fact in itself ought to suffice to undermine the myth of the "benign" *Duce* and his officials. In truth, however, what might have been explained away as a violent attempt to pacify a colony that had been rebellious for more than a decade proved to be the regime's routine modus operandi. "Frontier Fascism" applied methods of cultural annihilation systematically to destroy hostile ethnic groups: be it in the South Tyrol or along the eastern Adriatic, violence was used to impose the use of the Italian language and customs in mixed territories in which the contemporary presence of different ethnic groups had produced a unique border culture. The violence of ethnic assimilation arose from purely racist hatred in which the method used to combat the other was genocide.

For the German-speaking populations of Alto Adige, who enjoyed the dangerous protection of Hitler's Germany, a deportation plan was put in place, whereas for Slovenes and Croats, without the benefit of a watchful patron, concentration camps were opened during the war and practices were implemented in preparation for mass extermination.[18] Some historians calculate that in the Arbe concentration camp alone, opened in 1942, in little more than a year under the Italian regime, 35,000 Slovenes were imprisoned.[19] Others such as Filippo Focardi estimate that 25,000 Slovene citizens were deported during the period of military occupation. Calculating that 330,000 inhabitants were registered in the region, the figure amounts to 8 percent of the entire Slovene population.[20]

In this case too, the methods used for so-called "pacification" were thus deportation and extermination. It is no surprise therefore that some historians describe the Fascists' invasion of Yugoslavia as a "colonial undertaking."[21]

"He civilized the colonies and established by decree that they had the same rights and duties as Italians because they were ITALIANS!"

First "racist laws," then "racial laws"

Legislation obviously followed this way of interpreting the world: the laws of Fascism were racist long before 1938. As we have seen, the Colonial Code for Eritrea, which became the basis for the legislation for all Italy's colonial possessions, was already framed according to a distinction between European whites and colonized peoples. This approach was not only maintained but also tightened with the promulgation in 1933 of the Organic Legal System for Eritrea and Somalia,[22] which set out the guidelines for the racial identification of colonial subjects with clear reference to their subordination to whites. Article 15, for example, states that:

> "Eritrean or Somali subjects are: a) all individuals with residency in Eritrea or Italian Somalia and not Italian citizens or citizens of other states; b) individuals born of an Eritrean or Somali father or, in the event that the father is unknown, of an

Eritrean or Somali mother; c) individuals born in Eritrea or Somalia. In the event that both parents are unknown; d) a woman married to an Eritrean or Somali subject; e) an individual belonging to an African or Asian population who serves in a civilian or military capacity with the public administration in the colony or has served in this capacity and resides in the colony."

In practice, therefore, two basic characteristics were necessary to be colonial subjects: residency on the territory of the colony and the fact of not being white. The point that makes reference to Asians is particularly interesting: there were, in fact, colonies of Indian traders in particular throughout the Horn of Africa and their identity, which was neither white nor black, had to be made explicit according to the type of work they did.

This initial subdivision was important because it ensured that the colonial legislation was applied only to non-whites. Article 16 established that once someone was recognized as a colonial, they could only change citizenship with the governor's permission. This legislation was very useful when applied to nomad peoples, who the Italians wanted to rely on to exploit local resources. By restricting their right to movement, it ensured control over cheap labor for consolidated Italian businesses while, at the same time, destroying their millenary nomad culture.

Article 17 envisaged that "if someone is born in Eritrea or Italian Somalia of unknown parents, when physical features and any other evidence give reasonable grounds to believe that both parents were white, they are declared to be an Italian citizen." This means that the Fascist state evidently took care of abandoned children who were "certainly white," placing them under the protection of metropolitan law. The Fascists did not wish to abandon children of the ruling race and at the same time prevented confusion from arising among its colonial subjects.

Article 18 instead regulated access to application for Italian citizenship on reaching eighteen years of age to those who had "physical features and other evidence [that] give reasonable grounds to believe that one of their parents is white." To be eligible to make the application, the individual could not be polygamous or have a criminal record, and had to have passed the third elementary class promotion exam and had a "perfectly Italian" education. Acceptance of the application was nonetheless discretionary and entrusted to the unappealable judgment of the governor.

This racist impulse was neither cosmetic nor disregarded in the territories in which it was applied. Indeed, as the historian Nicola Labanca writes, "the institutionalization of racial dominance in the colonies was not limited to one law:

on the contrary, it availed itself of a diversified and pervasive production of laws."[23]

This general approach highlights two aspects of the Fascists' way of addressing the question of colonialism: the first is that, in the colonies, whites and non-whites had to have distinct social and administrative channels of their own, in a sort of apartheid Italian-style; the second is that, with ad hoc legislation, the Fascists pledged to defend the purity of the race from any possible contaminations. Italian citizenship was made impossible for anyone who had "mixed blood." The distinction imposed was clearly racial and is closely reminiscent of the genealogical methods applied by Nazi legislation to establish who was a Jew. But the so-called Nuremberg Laws on discrimination were only written in 1934, a year after the Italian colonial legislation had entered into force.

When the regime decided to attack Ethiopia in 1935, the subject of Fascist race and racism exploded in all its complexity. The propaganda had promised Italian soldiers "pretty Abyssinians" to conquer, with a clear allusion to the possibility of possessing them as sex objects. The war against Ethiopia was thus partly fueled by not overly disguised sexual enticement. This is why, once the country had been occupied, it is no wonder that unions between Italian men and African women became a problem for alleged

Italian racial purity, partly because in the aberrant conception of the "right of conquest," most of these so-called unions were nothing else but rape and concubinage imposed on local girls for the duration of the service of soldiers in the colony.

The phenomenon of mixed relationships grew in the course of the years to the extent that it ultimately jeopardized the regime's racist theories. The spread of practices such as *madamato*—an institution that effectively regulated temporary unions between local women and occupying soldiers—was curbed, not to guarantee the rights of concubines but to preserve the purity of the Italian race that Mussolini was seeking to forge. The effect of this policy of racial segregation did not put an end to unions, but it did represent a transition to more perfunctory, brutal practices. As the historian Giulietta Stefani writes, "These prohibitions led to the stigmatization, as opposed to the disappearance, of the *madamato* phenomenon. The climate of exacerbated racism and moral condemnation of interracial relations went on to provoke a resurgence of acts of violence by Italians against indigenous women."[24] The paradox of Mussolini's measures in the colonies was that even the minor legal and social protection provided for by the institution of *madamato* was removed, thus leaving women entirely at the mercy of the occupiers.

Seen through this lens, the promulgation of the anti-Jewish racial laws in 1938 acquires a broader, more complex significance than the one that revisionists seek to ascribe to it. The anti-Semitism that was made official by the racial laws was not the first step but just one of the many on Italian totalitarianism's racist journey: the choice to discriminate against the Jews was an obvious one insofar as all the other categories of possible opponents to the regime had already been eliminated or subdued. It was not critics of the regime who said this but the Grand Council of Fascism itself in a declaration that laid the bases for the laws. The preamble to the document, the official response to Fascist intellectuals' Manifesto of Race,[25] states that:

> "Following the conquest of the empire, the Grand Council of Fascism declares the urgent interest of racial problems and the need for a racial conscience. It points out that for sixteen years Fascism played and is still playing a positive role in the quantitative and qualitative improvement of the Italian race, an improvement that might be gravely compromised with incalculable political consequences by cross-breeding and bastardization. The Jewish problem is merely the metropolitan aspect of a problem of a general nature."[26]

The Grand Council's Declaration clarified the need to preserve the Italian race precisely at the moment in time, following the conquest of the empire, that it had become the Fascist race. When preparations were being made to unleash a racist offensive on Jews, it was not necessary, as many believe, to adopt the provisions enacted by the Nazis on the matter: there was already a whole battery of laws and rules that made the criteria of discrimination clear. This was accomplished, moreover, without any pressure from the Nazis.

It is sufficient to compare the above-cited formulas that were used to establish who was or was not a subject in the colonies with the criteria that established who, for Fascism, was a Jew. Article 8 of the decree law for the defense of the Italian race states that:

"In accordance with the law: a) anyone born of two Jewish parents, even if they belong to a religion other than the Jewish religion, is of Jewish race; b) anyone born of parents of whom one is of Jewish race and the other of foreign nationality is of Jewish race; c) anyone born of a Jewish mother is considered to be of Jewish race, if the father is unknown; d) anyone who, albeit born of parents of Italian nationality of whom only one is of Jewish race, belongs to the Jewish religion or is in any case registered in an Israelite community, or has in any other way made manifestations of Jewishness, is to be considered Jewish. Anyone born of parents of Italian nationality, of whom only one is of Jewish race, who, at the date of October 1, 1938-XVI [year on the Fascist calendar], belonged to a religion other than the Jewish religion, is not to be considered of Jewish race."[27]

This description has little in common with the framework of German laws that schematized a complicated genealogical axis and invented a new definition of what a Jew was from scratch.[28] The Fascist regime was thus able to follow the definitions contained in the racist laws it had already written for its African territories.

Another passage in the resolution of October 6, 1938, contains interesting parallels for comprehension of the regime's real behavior: "The Grand Council of Fascism does not exclude the possibility of granting, partly to divert Jewish immigration from Palestine, a controlled immigration of European Jews into some zones of Ethiopia. This possible condition and any others placed upon the Jews may be revoked or harshened according to the position Judaism assumes towards Fascist Italy."

This point in the resolution thus theorizes, at the highest level of government, the mass deportation of Jews outside the borders of the metropolitan state. It is a fundamental proposal that already sounds like a "final solution" to the Jewish question and has an evident precedent in the mass deportation of Arab and Berber populations in Graziani's Libya. Rereading these provisions today, the doubt arises as to who, Fascists or Nazis, was copying whom on the question.

*Did Mussolini protect the Jews in occupied territories
under Italian jurisdiction?*

One singular type of revisionism that is spreading across the web and the social media proposes a "conciliatory" version of Mussolini's regime, which, it is claimed, showed mercy to the Jews in France and the Balkans during the Italian occupation in World War II.

Archives from that period do report that, following Hitler's demand for Jewish refugees in southern France and certain areas of Yugoslavia be handed over, in 1941 the *Duce* personally gave orders to ignore it. For months, thousands of French and Yugoslav Jews evaded the concentration camps and remained under the protection of the Italian occupiers. For years, this act of apparent leniency served as the starting point for the posthumous rehabilitation of the regime and the building of the myth of anti-racist totalitarianism "Italian-style." What needs to be properly understood, however, is the reason for the gesture: in this case too, the basis for the Fascists' decisions was appearances.

By *ordering* its Italian allies to hand over the Jews, Hitler's Germany was virtually pretending to extend Nazi legislation to Fascist-occupied territories. The *Duce* refused to accept this clear manifestation of subservience not out of humanity but to score a point over his ally. More specifically, Mussolini had opened the Balkan front as a theater of war to demonstrate Italy's strategic independence, but the operation turned into an embarrassing military fiasco. Yielding to the extension of German racial legislation would therefore have been humiliating.

As the historian Filippo Focardi sums up, "Giving in to Croatia's and Germany's demands would have made Italy appear as a second-rate power and discredited the diplomatic and military authorities that, in September 1941, had promised protection to Jews and Serbians being hunted down by the Ustasha [the Croatian fascist militiamen who were allies of the Italians and Germans during the invasion of Yugoslavia]."[29] It was a matter of maintaining prestige but the problem ceased to exist a few months later, when there was no prestige left to maintain. As early as the summer of 1942, in fact, Mussolini officially agreed to the deportation of the Yugoslav Jews.[30] On the other hand, to give a clear picture of the regime's overall behavior towards the Jews, it is important to point out that, precisely in the Balkans, thousands of them were refused entry at the frontiers or denied protection by the Fascists, who were fully aware of the fate that awaited victims of persecution.[31]

An identical destiny met the French Jews who sought to flee from the fury of the Nazis by staying in the part of France occupied by the Italian army. They enjoyed a truce of a few months in the middle of a face-off triggered by a question of principle. When the principle ceased to exist, that is when the paucity of Fascist wishful thinking was unmasked, the Italian regime showed no particular scruples about collaborating in the extermination of European Jews. Indeed, rounding up Jews became routine practice for the Fascists of the Salò Republic, not because they were forced to by the Nazis but because it was no longer necessary to stress the differences that existed between the two regimes.

Contrary to what many like to think, Mussolini's racism had its own autonomy of thought and action: in some respects, it was a harbinger, and by no means a simple imitator, of the Nazi extermination plan. The 1938 laws are perfectly in line with the ideological drift of the regime, which began well before Hitler himself rose to power. Discrepancies in the application of laws between the two totalitarianisms were due, if anything, to the different situations in which they found themselves. With no colonies and still compromised by the restrictions imposed by the Treaty of Versailles, the Nazis concentrated immediately on their chief internal enemies, first their political opponents and then the Jews, who numbered just over half a million in Germany at the time. Fascism, focused as it was on the Mediterranean and keen to reconquer its colonies, concentrated its racial cleansing campaign on political opponents and colonial subjects before devoting itself to a numerically less important group such as that of Italian Jews (of whom there were fewer than 60,000 in 1938).

The development and application of the Italian racial laws, which were removed from public discourse and seen as a mere incidental detail not inherent to the dynamics of the regime, is a subject that has been confined to historians' debates for too long. But this way of repressing memory is dangerous because, as the historian David Bidussa wrote in 1994, "Failing to coming to terms with its anti-Semitism then, in the immediate post-war years, or in any case hurriedly by pursuing closure in the name of national reconciliation [...] entails the persistence of a common feeling which, if not opportunely monitored and controlled, could reopen the dynamic that the rhetoric of the post-World War II years dismissed as an ugly parenthesis that needed to be forgotten as a 'foreign body'."[32]

"Yet Mussolini was the politician who loved the Italians the most!"

It might be objected, however, that at least Mussolini's racism and violence were a phenomenon that developed outwards, not inwards against

Italian society. The forceful assertion above could have many meanings but it is, in general, not true, precisely because it was Italian citizens that the racial laws discriminated against. The intention of the people who say or write such sentences in the social media today is to mark a difference between Fascism, which is supposed to have had the destiny of Italians at heart, and the political class of today, which is seen as a whole as having only its own interests at heart.

Getting down to facts, as far as the *Duce*'s love of his people is concerned, one notes that, as Mussolini himself admitted, it was more of a "love-hate" relationship: what he regarded as the ineptitude, stupidity and untrustworthiness of the Italians, especially at the beginning and end of his own political trajectory—that is, when they bent with lesser zeal to his will—are themes that recurred often in his more or less private conversations. As Ciano wrote in his diary: "January 29, 1940 [...] the *Duce* is irritated by the internal situation. The people grumble. Food restrictions are a matter to be taken into account. War again casts its shadow on the country. ... [for the *Duce*] ... the Italian race is a race of sheep. Eighteen years are not enough to change them. It takes a hundred and eighty, and maybe a hundred and eighty centuries."[33]

When the Greek offensive came to a standstill, on December 23, 1940, Ciano noted that,

"Then speaking of the rather indifferent behavior of our troops, he added, 'I must nevertheless recognize that the Italians of 1914 were better than these. It is not flattering for the regime, but that's the way it is.'"

The following day, Christmas Eve 1940, the leader's judgment was even more severe: "It's snowing. The *Duce* looks out the window and is glad that it is snowing. 'This snow and cold are very good,' he says. 'In this way our good-for-nothing men and this mediocre race will be improved.'"[34]

On many occasions in which Mussolini's aspirations and the real capabilities of his people did not coincide, the dictator was quick to lay the blame for failure on the Italians. As De Felice sums up, "After the early years of the regime, Mussolini soon reached the conviction that, although Fascism had opened and indicated a road and a destination for Italy, the Italians lacked the 'character' needed to be truly Fascist [...] The *Duce* felt that the only thing to do at that point was to transform the Italian people and, above all, create new generations, more numerous, physically stronger and morally Fascist, truly capable of 'daring' and entering into action."[35]

For years, the regime sought to delve into the lives and minds of Italians through the education system, the destruction of dissent and the militarization of the masses, but with very mediocre results. At the moment in which Mussolini realized that he would be unable to "fascisize" a whole people, he began to despise that people and consider it unsuited to achieving the great things he had planned for it. This essentially eugenic vision of the challenges that the regime forced on the nation led to political choices in which the value of single lives was irrelevant. The famous phrase Mussolini is said to have uttered at the onset of the Second World War—"I only need a few thousand dead so that I can sit at the peace conference as a man who has fought"— gives the measure of his consideration for his own people. The Italians incapable of becoming the new men he had hoped so much to see would at least serve as cannon fodder for the greater glory of the Fascist ideal.

In addition to the contempt for the Italians that Mussolini accumulated over the years, it is worth remembering the concrete actions that the Fascists took to change their way of life. The Fascist regime was responsible for the greatest limitation of the civil rights of Italians since the concept of civil rights had come into existence.

Every manifestation of free civil life took a step backwards: the rights to vote and to assemble freely were removed, and the public expression of ideas was censored, not only in the media but also in private correspondence. The police apparatus grew out of all proportion, suggesting that if the *Duce* loved his people, he certainly did not trust them. Fascism also created a certain idea of social fracture among Italians: the obligation to be a party member to hold public office[36]—namely to be a prefect—was extended to most of society from 1926[37] to build what was, to all intents and purposes, a legal and rights distinction between ordinary Italians and Fascist Italians. These measures, which limited citizens' freedom of expression and left the provincial party secretary to decide whether they were eligible to hold Fascist positions, demonstrate that the dictatorship was structurally discriminatory towards Italians themselves.

If loving Italians meant making them happy, Fascism, as we have seen, failed on both the economic and the social fronts.

If loving Italians meant defending their honor, the behavior of the "new Italians" the regime boasted about in Africa, Spain, Russia, the Balkans and all the theaters of war in which the Fascist method of fighting was applied, would be enough not only to raise doubts about the "honor of Fascist arms" but would also require all Italian society today to make a searching reassessment of its memory of that period. The historian Filippo Focardi recalls that:

> The United Nations War Crime Commission inscribed in the list of presumed war criminals to put on trial 729 Italian servicemen and civilians wanted by Yugoslavia, 111 by Greece, nine

by France and three by Albania. Soon after the Italian peace treaty came into force, Yugoslavia had followed diplomatic channels to forward directly to Rome requests for the extradition of 45 Italians (some of whom already present in the international lists), while Greece in turn had made a request for 74 names (some of which also in United Nations lists), Albania for 142 and France for 30. Ethiopia too accused ten Italians (later to limit its requests to Rodolfo Graziani and Pietro Badoglio),* while the Soviet Union had demanded the consignment of twelve Italians accused of war crimes as early as 1944. None of them were extradited, however.[38]

If loving Italians meant protecting them, Fascism involved the country in a war that, according to Italian Ministry of Defense estimates in 1957, caused 472,000 Italian deaths, a third of whom were civilians.

To these must be added the Italian victims of *squadrista* violence, deaths in prison and internal exile and soldiers killed in the wars of aggression in Ethiopia and domination of Libya, but also the deaths caused by the precarious sanitary conditions in the country under the regime. The

---

* Pietro Badoglio (1871–1956) was an Italian general who fought in both World Wars, serving as first viceroy of Italian East Africa in between. Following the armistice and the fall of the Fascist regime on September 1943, he became Prime Minister of Italy, a position he held for nine months until the capture of Rome by the Allies. (translator's note)

total exceeds the numbers of Italian deaths in any other historical event and makes the Fascist period the deadliest in the history of the country. If ever there was an attempted systemic genocide of the Italian people, it was perpetrated, more or less consciously, by Fascist tyranny.

Assorted Information (and Idiocies)

Everything you always wanted to know about the *Duce* ... that actually turns out to be false

The great mystifications presented above concern primarily the relationship between Fascism and Italian society. They were typical of the immediate post-regime years and have long entered the debate on the lies that eddy around about the historiography of the Fascist period. However, urban legends have recently begun to proliferate on the web about presumed behavior of Mussolini and the Fascists that are in clear contrast with those of the politicians of today. The underlying aim of this fake news is to make a comparison between then and now, and to create the classic effect of nostalgia for a purely imaginary past.

Here are some examples of stories that have been invented around the figure of Mussolini and have spread over the years.

"When He was around, trains arrived on time."

Arguably the most famous of the revisionist claims. And to be fair, it does contain a grain of truth: under Fascism there was no talk at all of trains being late.

When the regime began to exert close control over information in the country with its first newspaper law in 1925,[1] which placed all news about public life under surveillance. As the years went by, the regime tightened its grip and meddled in aspects of daily life that were not strictly political. For example, the passing of the public safety law Consolidation Act in 1931[2] made official the concept of "offence to the prestige of the state or authority or offensive to the feeling of the nation."[3] This definition obviously comprised all the news that, according to the authorities, might constitute an insult to the state's prestige.

This vast field, which was entrusted to the judgment of provincial police chiefs, encompassed all news regarded as being defeatist: not only mismanagement of public affairs, scandals, government failings but also unsolved crimes, insofar as they showed the police in a bad light, and any inefficiency on the part of the public sector, such as dysfunctions in the health service and—the case in point—trains arriving late.

"When He was around, ministers rode bikes without escorts."

There is no evidence of measures obliging ministers to keep this kind of low profile. On the contrary, there are many accounts of ministers and *gerarchi*, Fascist Party bosses, exploiting their positions to live in luxury. One example was Italo Balbo, an air force flying ace who used his plane even for the briefest journeys and ordered airports to prepare special runways for him whenever he was traveling around Italy in an official capacity. Mussolini himself made short domestic journeys by air, even to travel to his native Romagna region from Rome for the weekend. In general, the regime was never a lover of sustainable mobility. In the 1930s, in order to boost sales of the industrialist Agnelli's cars, Mussolini even levied a road tax on bicycles and animal-drawn vehicles.[4]

"Mussolini imposed equal rights for people and animals."

A relatively recent example of fake news has arisen in the wake of growing interest for animal rights. Leaving aside the difficulty of understanding what "giving equal rights" to animals and human beings means, the only proof of the assertion may be found in Fascist legislation, which was however framed for an entirely different purpose. Indeed, Royal Decree 1175 of 1931[5] set limitations on keeping animals, especially dogs, in urban centers, and even introduced a tax for dog owners, more specifically "150 lire for luxury breeds and pet (companion) dogs, 50 lire for hunting and guard dogs, 15 lire for dogs trained to watch buildings or herd sheep for commercial purposes."

"Everybody knows but nobody says it! In 1929 Benito Mussolini imposed equal rights for humans and dogs, man's best friend, and every young person was entrusted with a dog to learn the values of brotherhood, compassion and cohesion."

"Mussolini allowed Italians to have more children and made the Italian population grow."

This claim seems to be supported by censuses of the population resident in Italy, which increased from 38,449,000 in 1921 to 42,994,000 in 1936 (the last census available for the Fascist period).[6]

The population growth dynamic, however, depended not on increased possibilities for having children or the regime's policies to raise the birth rate but simply on the fact that it was harder for Italians to emigrate under the Fascists. In 1923, 389,000 Italians left the country, whereas on the eve of World War II, in 1939, the number had dropped to 29,000.[7] The slump was caused by the international Depression that led destination countries to close their borders and by the policies to discourage emigration introduced by the regime. Seeking fortune abroad was seen as a national disgrace.[8] On account of the privations and the ongoing crisis, the actual fertility rate during Fascism shrank from 30.54 children born for every one thousand inhabitants in 1921 to 22.40 in 1936.[9]

"Mussolini placed Italy at the forefront of scientific discovery."

It is hard to establish what this statement means exactly. If we begin with international awards in the field, as is often the criterion adopted, the three Italian Nobel Prize winners who lived during Fascism come to mind: Guglielmo Marconi, Luigi Pirandello and Enrico Fermi. For different reasons, all three had relations with the regime. Marconi won the Nobel Prize for physics in 1909, when Mussolini was still a young socialist, thanks among other things to his education and experiments in Great Britain and United States. When the Fascists took power, they praised Marconi as an Italian glory, and through their propaganda appropriated results achieved long before the March on Rome.

Enrico Fermi won the Nobel Prize, again for physics, in 1938, but after receiving it in Stockholm, fled to the United States to save his Jewish wife Laura from the racial laws. It was thus impossible for Mussolini to take the credit.

Pirandello, who won the Nobel Prize for literature in 1934, is a case apart. He was a member of the Fascist Party in that period and was sensitive to the idea of becoming one of the fetishes the regime liked to display abroad for its own glorification. But he discovered almost at once that appearing in the showcase of Fascism also meant losing independence and being subject to controls and censorship. Before he died in 1936, he made a public statement refusing any posthumous honor that might be bestowed by the government. This public demonstration of aversion provoked an outburst of international indignation and sharp embarrassment among Mussolini's entourage.

These cases apart, if we really wish to measure the regime's impact on the development of science in Italy, all that is necessary is a close look at the data. Because of the Gentile reform, which strongly oriented the Italian education system towards classical subjects, the number of Italians actively involved in scientific and technical learning dropped. And after the launch of the reform, the number of students at polytechnical and science faculties dropped too. As the "Fascism and Science" entry in the *Enciclopedia Treccani* says, "If in the 1921-22 academic year students enrolled on scientific degree courses represented more than 60 per cent of the total, in 1939-40 it was students of classical subjects who constituted 66 per cent. Particularly conspicuous in the science area was the decrease in the number of engineering students, which fell in absolute terms from 11,423 in 1921-22 to 7,818 in 1939-40."[10]

Acknowledgments

One warm morning in early summer the conversation turned to the sad battles that are being fought out in the social media between the *Duce*'s admirers and detractors, gory conflicts in which insults and what pass as arguments are exchanged. "When they start going on about pensions and land reclamation, the blood goes to my head! What we need is a book collecting and exposing all this fake news, that way they'd stop telling lies about Fascism!" Here it is, Giosuè. They probably won't stop anyway, but at least it's a start. My first thank-you goes to you and those like you who are still keen to stem false news about one of the twentieth century's most evil regimes.

Thanks to Cristina, who stuck a note on the board in our kitchen in which the phrase that Nora Joyce used to repeat to her husband James— "Why don't you write sensible books that people can understand"—read like a warning. Thanks to my family for their support and suggestions: this book is partly the fruit of furious debates over Christmas dinners.

My heartfelt thanks go to my friend Carlo Greppi, who fell in love with the project immediately and performed, as the need arose, as friend, critic, agent, fan and detractor. Thanks also to Michele Luzzatto who, with attention, passion and experience, guided the construction of these pages.

Thanks to Lorenzo Bigiarini, historian and fellow traveler, for revising the text and for the popularization work he has been doing for years. Thanks to Jessica Ognibeni, a friend, a historian and a precious hunter of books and of typos. Thanks to Alice Ravinale for her inestimable prompts and suggestions when the work was under way. Thanks to David Bidussa for our conversations in the snow and for admitting that he enjoyed reading me.

Thanks to the whole wonderful team at the Deina Association, the friends who over the last few years have traveled part of the way together, working on history as a reservoir of memory from which we can fish a better future—a reservoir whose water we all hope will stay limpid. The journeys, the discussions and the influences received in the places in which the twentieth century showed itself at its worst were and are the most precious part of the work we share. This book is intended as a small piece in the great mosaic of our reflection which, I feel sure, will grow in the years to come. So a heartfelt thanks, in strictly alphabetical order, to Sara Bagnoli, Matteo Balduzzi, Elena Bissaca, Filippo Bonadiman, Sofia Burioli, Gianluca Corzani, Alessandro Huber, Cristina Lentini, Francesca Poli, Davide Toso, Antonio Trombetta and all Deina's team of tutors: there are more than a hundred of you and the publisher said I couldn't mention you all!

Last but not least, thanks to all the thousands of participants in the "journeys of memory" I have met on my travels in the last few years. Thanks because you have chosen to do something that is wonderfully useful, albeit terribly unfashionable: stopping and taking time to reflect.

Bibliography

Various authors, *Storia dell'IRI*, Laterza, Rome-Bari 2012.

E. Bartocci (ed.), *Una stagione del riformismo*, Fondazione Giacomo Brodolini, Rome 2010.

P. Bianchi, *La rincorsa frenata. L'industria italiana dall'unità nazionale all'unificazione europea*, il Mulino, Bologna 2002.

D. Bidussa, *Il mito del bravo italiano*, il Saggiatore, Milan 1994.

M. Bloch, 'Reflections of a Historian on the False News of the War (trans. James P. Holoka), in *Michigan War Studies Review*, vol. 2013-051, Eastern Michigan University, Ypsilanti 2013.

A. Burgio, L. Casali (eds), *Studi sul razzismo italiano*, Clueb, Bologna 1996.

I. Campbell, *The Addis Ababa Massacre: Italy's National Shame*, C. Hurst & Co. Publishers, London 2017.

M. Canali, *Il delitto Matteotti*, il Mulino, Bologna 2015.

M. L. Cavalcanti, *La politica monetaria italiana fra le due guerre (1918-1943)*, Franco Angeli, Milan 2011.

F. L. Cavallo, *Terre, acque, macchine. Geografia della bonifica in Italia tra Ottocento e Novecento*, Diabasis, Parma 2011.

E. Ciconte, *Storia Criminale. La resistibile ascesa di mafia, 'ndrangheta e camorra dall'Ottocento ai giorni nostri*, Rubbettino, Palermo 2008.

E. Collotti, *Il fascismo e gli ebrei*, Laterza, Rome-Bari 2004.

G. Corni, *Storia della Germania. Da Bismarck alla Merkel*, il Saggiatore, Milano 2017.

A. Del Boca, *Italiani, Brava gente? Un mito duro a morire*, Neri Pozza, Vicenza 2005.

R. De Felice, *Mussolini il rivoluzionario* (1883-1920), Einaudi, Turin 2018.

R. De Felice, *Mussolini il fascista. La conquista del potere* (1921-1925), Einaudi, Turin 1995.

R. De Felice, *Mussolini il fascista. L'organizzazione dello Stato fascista (1925-1929)*, Einaudi, Turin 1995.

R. De Felice, *Mussolini il duce. Gli anni del consenso (1929-1936)*, Einaudi, Turin 1995.

V. De Grazia, *How Fascism Ruled Women*, University of California Press, Berkeley 2007.

C. Di Sante, *Italiani senza onore. I crimini in Jugoslavia e i processi negati, 1941-1951*, Ombre Corte, Verona 2005.

P. Dogliani, *Il fascismo degli italiani. Una storia sociale*, UTET, Turin 2014.

U. Eco, 'Ur-Fascism' in *How To Spot A Fascist* (trans. Alastair McEwen, Richard Dixon), Harvill Secker, London 2020.

F. Focardi, *Il cattivo tedesco e il bravo italiano. La rimozione delle colpe della seconda guerra mondiale*, Laterza, Rome-Bari 2013.

M. Franzinelli, *I tentacoli dell'OVRA. Agenti, collaboratori e vittime della polizia politica fascista*, Bollati Boringhieri, Turin 2000.

M. Franzinelli, M. Magnani, *Beneduce, il finanziere di Mussolini*, Mondadori, Milan 2009.

M. Franzinelli, *Il Prigioniero di Salò*, Mondadori, Milan 2012.

M. Franzinelli, *Delatori, spie e confidenti anonimi. L'arma segreta del regime fascista*, Feltrinelli, Milan 2012.

G. Galeotti, *Storia del voto alle donne in Italia. Alle radici del difficile rapporto tra donne e politica*, Biblink, Rome 2006.

E. Gentile, *Fascismo di pietra*, Laterza, Rome-Bari 2007.

E. Gentile, *Mussolini e il Fascismo*, Laterza, Rome-Bari 2010.

E. Gentile, S. M. Di Scala, *Mussolini socialista*, Laterza, Rome-Bari 2015.

H. Gibson (ed.), *The Ciano Diaries, 1939-1943: The Complete and Unabridged Diaries of Count Galeazzo Ciano, Italian Minister for Foreign Affairs, 1936-1943*, Simon Publications, New York 1945.

Paul Ginsborg, *A History of Contemporary Italy: Society and Politics 1943-1988*, Penguin Books, London 1990, p. 215.

P. Giovannini, M. Palla, *Il fascismo dalle mani sporche. Dittatura, corruzione affarismo*, Laterza, Rome-Bari 2019.

C. Greppi, *25 aprile 1945*, Laterza, Rome-Bari 2018.

F. Guarneri, *Battaglie economiche fra le due guerre*, il Mulino, Bologna 1988.

R. J. Kipling, *Collected Poems*, Wordsworth Editions, London 1994.

N. Labanca, *Oltremare. Storia dell'espansione coloniale italiana*, il Mulino, Bologna 2007.

S. La Francesca, *La politica economica del fascismo*, Laterza, Bari 1973.

S. Lupo, *Storia della mafia. Dalle origini ai nostri giorni*, Donzelli, Roma 2004.

L. Martone, *Giustizia coloniale. Modelli e prassi penali per i sudditi d'Africa dall'età giolittiana al fascismo*, Jovene Editore, Naples 2002.

S. Martorelli, P. Zani (eds), *Una piccola storia della previdenza in Italia*, CISL, Milan 2010.

G. Melis, *La macchina imperfetta. Immagine e realtà dello Stato fascista*, il Mulino Bologna 2018.

P. Milza, *Gli ultimi giorni di Mussolini*, Longanesi, Milan 2011.

G. Mosse, The Crisis of German Ideology, H. Fertig, New York 1998,

E. Novello, *La bonifica in Italia. Legislazione, credito e lotta alla malaria dall'unità al fascismo*, Franco Angeli, Milan 2003.

G. Oliva, *Si ammazza troppo poco. I crimini di guerra italiani, 1940- 1943*, Mondadori, Milan 2007.

A. Petacco, *L'archivio segreto di Mussolini*, Mondadori, Milan 2010.

R. Petri, *Storia economica d'Italia dalla Grande guerra al miracolo economico (1918-1963)*, il Mulino, Bologna 2002.

G. Rochat, *Guerre italiane (1935-1943). Dall'Impero d'Etiopia alla disfatta*, Einaudi, Turin 2008.

D. Rodogno, *Il nuovo ordine mediterraneo. Le politiche di occupazione dell'Italia fascista in Europa (1940-1943)*, Bollati Boringhieri, Turin 2003.

J. Roth, *La quarta Italia*, Lit Edizioni, Roma 2013.

G. Salvemini, *The Origins of Fascism in Italy*, Harper & Row, New York 1973.

A. Sangiovanni, *Le parole e le figure. Storia dei media italiani dall'età libera alle seconda guerra mondiale.* Donzelli, Rome 2012.

U. Santino, *Storia del movimento antimafia*, Editori Riuniti, Rome 2000.

F. Scarano, *Tra Mussolini e Hitler. Le opzioni dei sudtirolesi nella politica estera fascista*, Franco Angeli, Milan 2012.

D.M. Smith, *A proposito di Mussolini*, Laterza, Rome-Bari 2004.

D.M. Smith, *Mussolini, A Biography*, Knopf, New York 1982.

F. M. Snowden, The Conquest of Malaria. Italy 1900-1962, Yale University Press, New Haven 2008.

G. Stefani, *Colonia per maschi. Italiani in Africa orientale: una storia di genere*, Ombre Corte, Verona 2007.

A. Tasca, *Nascita e avvento del fascismo*, Laterza, Roma-Bari 1972.

T. Terhoeven, *Oro alla Patria. Donne, guerra e propaganda nella giornata della fede fascista*, il Mulino, Bologna 2006.

G. Toniolo, *L'Italia e l'economia mondiale. Dall'Unità a oggi*, Marsilio, Venice 2013.

L. Teoldi, *Storia dello Stato italiano. Dall'Unità al XXI secolo*, Laterza, Rome-Bari 2018.

G. Vecchi, *In ricchezza e in povertà. Il benessere degli italiani dall'Unità a oggi*, il Mulino, Bologna 2011.

Literature

G. Bassani, *The Gold-Rimmed Spectacles*, Penguin Classics, London 2012. B. Fenoglio, *A Private Affair*, Hesperus, London 2006. E. Flaiano, *A Time to Kill*, Quartet Books, London 2003, A. Scurati, *M. Son of the Century*, Fourth Estate, London 2021, A. Pennachi, *The Mussolini Canal*, Dedalus, Sawtry (UK). R. Viganò, *L'Agnese va a morire*, Einaudi, Turin 2014.

Film

Over the years many films have tried to tell the story of Fascism and its real relationship with Italy. This tough challenge, which has not always been achieved, has focused on various aspects of the regime. Some masterpieces, such as *Amarcord* (Federico Fellini, 1973), have been more revelatory than others, exposing and making fun of the more grotesque aspects of the farcical regime, its vainglory and its empty pompousness. The impact of the choices and non-choices of Mussolini's regime on the lives of individuals is reflected in the character played by Marcello Mastroianni in *A Special Day* (Ettore Scola, 1977). The suffering of marginalised human beings under the regime is portrayed in *Christ Stopped in Eboli* (Francesco Rosi, 1979). The tragic irony of a regime that wasn't a farce but a veritable tragedy is conveyed by Massimo Troisi's fantastic performance in *The Ways of the Lord are Over* (Massimo Troisi, 1987). A film that analyses language and non-language of Fascism and its most risible idiosyncracies is the science-fiction comedy *Fascisti su Marte* (Fascists On Mars) (Corrado Guzzanti, 2006), in which the regime's tedious rhetoric is exposed in a perfect demonstration of how Italian totalitarianism was never able to turn its façade into reality.

Online sources for fact checking

Legislation:

normattiva.it (a collection of Italian legal production from 1861 to the present day).

augusto.agid.gov.it (a collection of the digitalized historical data sets of the *Gazzetta ufficiale 1861-1946*).

Economics:

seriestoriche.istat.it (statistical indexes from 1861 to the present day).

Health:

politichesanitarie.it

Mafia:

centroimpastato.com

legislature.camera.it/_bicamerali/antimafia/sportello/collegamenti.html (list of Mafia and anti-Mafia sites compiled by the Bicameral Anti-Mafia Commission).

Natural Calamities:

protezionecivile.gov.it

storing.ingv.it (the site of the National Institute of Geology and Volcanology).

Social Insurance:

inps.it

Notes

Preface. Did Mussolini do any good at all?

1. M. Bloch, 'Reflections of a Historian on the False News of the War (trans. James P. Holoka), in *Michigan War Studies Review*, vol. 2013-051, Eastern Michigan University, Ypsilanti, MI 2013.

2 U. Eco, 'Ur-Fascism' in *How To Spot A Fascist* (trans. Alastair McEwen, Richard Dixon), Harvill Secker, London 2020.

Chapter 1. Mussolini the Provident and Prudential

1. 'Alters - und Invaliditätsversicherung', cf. G. Corni, *Storia della Germania: da Bismarck alla Merkel*, il Saggiatore, Milan 2017, p. 68.

2. Royal Decree no. 70 of 21 February 1895 in approval of the Consolidated Act on civil and military pension laws. In *Gazzetta Ufficiale* no. 70 of 23/3/1895.

3. Law no. 350 of July 17, 1898, instituting a National Workers' Invalidity and Retirement Fund. In *Gazzetta Ufficiale* no.186 of 11/8/1898.

4. Lieutenant Decree Law no. 603 of April 21, 1919, concerning compulsory insurance against invalidity and old age for people of both sexes employed by others. In *Gazzetta Ufficiale* no.104 of 1/5/1919, converted by Law no. 47317 of April 1925, in In *Gazzetta Ufficiale* no. 104 of 5/5/1925.

5. Royal Decree no. 915 of April 27, 1923, abolishing the Ministry of Labor and Welfare. In *Gazzetta Ufficiale* no. 106 of 5/5/1923.

6. G. Melis, *La macchina imperfetta. Immagine e realtà dello Stato fascista*, il Mulino, Bologna 2018, p. 449.

7. Royal Decree no. 3158 of 30 December 1923, Obligatory insurance against involuntary unemployment. Assicurazione obbligatoria contro la disoccupazione involontaria. In *Gazzetta Ufficiale* no. 34 of 9/2/1924.

8. Royal Decree Law no. 2055 of 30 October 1927, Obligatory insurance against tuberculosis. In *Gazzetta Ufficiale* no. 265 of 16/11/1927, converted by Law no. 20 of May 1928, in *Gazzetta Ufficiale* no.134 of 9/6/1928.

9. INPS, Minutes of the meeting of the Executive Committee of February 22, 1924, in G. Melis, *La macchina imperfetta.*, cit., p. 451.

10. Royal Decree Law no. 371 of March 1933, n. 371, Coordination of the organs of administration of the National Social Insurance which assumes the name of "Fascist National Insurance Institute". In *Gazzetta Ufficiale* no. 106 of 6/5/1933, converted by Law no. 166 of January 3, 1934, in *Gazzetta Ufficiale* no. 43 of 21/2/1934.

11. G. Melis, *La macchina imperfetta.*, cit., p. 463.

12. G. Melis, *La macchina imperfetta.*, cit. p. 464.

13. Law no. 782 of May 29, 1939, Recruitment of members of Fascist action squads in state administration offices and other public bodies. In *Gazzetta Ufficiale* no. 43 of 21/2/1934, converted by Law no. 166 of January 3, 1934, in *Gazzetta Ufficiale* no. 43 of 21/2/1934.

14. Royal Decree Law no. 704 of August 2, 1943, Abolition of the Fascist National Party. In *Gazzetta Ufficiale* no. 180 of 5/8/1943, converted by Law no. 5 of May 5, 1949, in *Gazzetta Ufficiale* no. 105 of 7/5/1949.

15. Law no. 153 of April 30, 1969, Revision of the pension system and social security legislation. In *Gazzetta Ufficiale* no. 111 of 30/4/1969.

16. Cf. 'Tredicesima,' entry in *Enciclopedia Treccani*, www.treccani.it.

17. *"Mille lire al mese"* (A Thousand Lire A Month), sung by Gilberto Mazzi, was released in 1939 and was one of Italy's biggest hits at the time. The lyrics are, significantly, a hymn to the pursuit of economic security and tranquillity. The chorus goes, "If only I could have a thousand lire a month/

without exaggerating/I'd be sure to find/total happiness/A modest job/I'm easy to please/I want to work/to eventually find/total tranquility." In 1939 a steady job was still the Italian dream but the dream often gave way to simply getting by in a dignified manner, something that was evidently not within everybody's reach. As Andrea Sangiovanni explains in his *Le parole e le figure*, "These are lyrics in which, between the lines, it is possible to detect the consequences of the economic crisis and sanctions." Cf. A. Sangiovanni, *Le parole e le figure. Storia dei media italiani dall'età libera alla seconda guerra mondiale*, Donzelli, Rome 2012, p. 200.

18. Cf. National Collective Labor Agreement, in *Gazzetta Ufficiale* no. 199 of 27/8/1937.

19. Decree of the President of the Republic no. 1070 of July 28, 1960, Rules and regulations governing the wages of workers employed in industrial enterprises. In *Gazzetta Ufficiale* ordinary supplement no. 2480 of 10/10/1960.

20. Legislative Decree of the Provisional Head of State no. 869 of August 12, 1947, New provisions on wage supplements. In *Gazzetta Ufficiale* no. 210 of 12/9/1947.

21. Law no. 563 of April 3, 1926, n. 563, Rules and regulations governing collective wage agreements. In *Gazzetta Ufficiale* no. 87 of 14/4/1926.

22. On the real effect of the application of Fascist corporative theories, cf. G. Melis, *La macchina imperfetta.*, cit. p. 464.

23. Royal Decree no. 113 of July 22, 1926, Abrogation of the industrial regulation in force in the new Provinces and provisions for its coordination by Law no. 563 of April 3, 1926, on the legal control of collective labor agreements. In *Gazzetta Ufficiale* no. 155 del 7/7/1926.

24. Law no. 129 of January 19, 1939, Institution of the Chambers of Fasces and Corporations. In *Gazzetta Ufficiale* no. 37 of 14/2/1926.

25. G. Melis, *La macchina imperfetta.*, cit., pp. 304-05.

26. E. Gentile, *Fascismo, Storia e interpretazione*, Laterza, Rome-Bari 2018, p. 27.

Chapter 2. Mussolini the Champion of Land Reclamation

1. For the historical context of the situation in Italy's marshlands in the second half of the nineteenth century, cf. E. Novello, *La bonifica in Italia. Legislazione, credito e lotta alla malaria dall'unità al fascismo*, Franco Angeli, Milan 2003.

2. Law no. 4642 of December 11, 1878, concerning the reclamation of the Agro romano. In *Gazzetta Ufficiale* no. 301 of 23/12/1878.

3. Royal Decree no. 647 of November 10, 1905, in approval of the Consolidated Act on the reclamation of the Agro romano and the colonization of state property. In *Gazzetta Ufficiale* no. 102 of 1/5/1906.

4. Royal Decree no. 3256 of December 30, 1923, Consolidated Act on the marsh and marshland reclamation laws. In *Gazzetta Ufficiale* no. 71 of 24/3/1924.

5. F. L. Cavallo, Terre, acque, macchine. Geografia della bonifica in Italia tra Ottocento e Novecento, Diabasis, Parma 2011, p. 100.

6. Royal Law by Decree no. 1606 of September 16, 1928, in approval of the legislative regulation for the organization and functions of the National Veterans Association. In *Gazzetta Ufficiale* no. 220 of 22/9/1926, converted by Law no. 110 of June 6 1927, in *Gazzetta Ufficiale* no. 157 of 9/7/1927.

7. Cf. Royal Decree Law no. 1606 of September 16, 1928, art. 2. In *Gazzetta Ufficiale* no. 220 of 22/9/1926.

8. Law no. 3134 of December 24, 1928, Provisions for integral reclamation. In *Gazzetta Ufficiale* no. 12 of 15/1/1929.

9. R. De Felice, *Mussolini il duce. Gli anni del consenso (1929-1934)*, Einaudi, Turin 1996, p. 144.

10. "The allocation of 257 million lire will stay unchanged for every fiscal year from 1944 to 1959-60, decreasing in subsequent fiscal years in relation to the gradual expenditure of the annual sums over the next thirty years." Cf. Law no. 3134 of December 24, art. 2. In *Gazzetta Ufficiale* no. 12 of 15/1/1929.

11. Cf. ISTAT historical data sets. In 1928 the total area of farming land and woodland was 27,196,000 hectares. In seriestoriche.istat.it.

12. R. Petri, *Storia economica d'Italia. Dalla Grande Guerra al miracolo econo-mico (1918-1963)*, il Mulino, Bologna 2002, p. 252.

13. "Even though,"as Emilio Gentile points out apropos the myth of *Romanità*, the Roman spirit, "correspondence between Fascist *Romanità* with the Roman historical model was in many cases arbitrary, imaginary or simply inexistent." Cf. E. Gentile, *Fascismo di pietra*, Laterza, Roma-Bari 2007, p. 52.

14. Royal Decree no. 215 of February 13, 1933, New rules and regulations for integral reclamation. In *Gazzetta Ufficiale* no. 79 of 4/4/1933.

15. E. Novello, *La bonifica in Italia*, cit., p. 280.

16. R. De Felice, *Mussolini il duce*, cit., p. 146.

17. The data on malaria presented here are taken from seriestoriche.istat.it, Salubrity and Health, Table 4.15 – Reported cases of diseases whose reporting was compulsory - Years 1925-2009 (absolute totals per 100,000 inhabitants) and Table 4.15.1 - Reported cases of diseases whose reporting was compulsory - Years 1888-1924 (absolute totals per 100,000 inhabitants).

18. ISTAT historical data sets, consultable on line in seriestoriche.istat.it.

19. Ministry of Health, "*Profilassi della malaria, introduzione,*" in salute.gov.it.

Chapter 3. Mussolini the Builder

1. In 2017, 79.9 per cent of Italian families owned the house they were living in. Cf. "*Condizioni economiche delle famiglie-condizioni abitative*" in istat.it.

2. "Art. 47. The Republic shall encourage and protect savings in all forms. It shall regulate, co-ordinate and oversee credit activities. The Republic shall promote house and farm ownership and direct and indirect shareholding in major national enterprises through the use of private savings." Constitution of the Italian Republic. Senato della Repubblica, Rome 2018.

3. ISTAT historical data sets, *"Popolazione residente e bilancio demografico ai confini dell'epoca* (1862-1947)," in seriestoriche.istat.it.

4. Law no. 254 of May 31, 1903, n. 254, On social housing. In *Gazzetta Ufficiale*, no.159 of 8/7/1903.

5. Ibid., art. 2.

6. Among the first were those made in Bari by Royal Decree no. 241 of June 7, 1906, In *Gazzetta Ufficiale*, no.172 of 24/7/1906 and in Bologna by Royal Decree no. 237 of July 8 of 1906, in *Gazzetta Ufficiale*, no.169 of 20/7/1906.

7. Institutes were required to inscribe rules and regulations "stating in their statutes that the shareholders' annual dividend cannot exceed 4 per cent of the effectively paid up capital and that, in the event of reimbursement or payment, cannot be distributed among the shareholders, for whatever reason, a sum that exceeds by more than a fifth the total of the capital repaid or paid in insofar as residual assets must be allocated to the National Workers' Invalidity and Retirement Fund," in *Gazzetta Ufficiale* no. 159 of 8/7/1903, art. 2.

8. Royal Decree no. 516 of December 8, 1907, Establishment as a moral body. In *Gazzetta Ufficiale* no. 304 del 26/12/1907

9. Royal Decree no. 356 of 17 July 1908, Reflecting statute approval. *Gazzetta Ufficiale* no. 225 del 26/9/1908.

10. Royal Decree no. 360 of 12 August 1908, Reflecting establishment as a moral body. In *Gazzetta Ufficiale* no. 227 of 29/9/1908.

11. Royal Decree no. 528 of August 12, 1908, Approving the regulations for the execution of Law (Consolidated Act) no. 89 of February 27, 1908, or social or economic housing. In *Gazzetta Ufficiale* no. 222 of 23/9/1908.

12. Law no. 1129 of June 6, 1935, Rules and regulations for the reform of social housing Institutes and the constitution of a national Consortium of the aforesaid Institutes. In *Gazzetta Ufficiale* no. 156 of 6/7/1935.

13. P. di Biagi (ed.), *La grande ricostruzione. Il piano Ina-Casa e l'Italia degli anni cinquanta*, Donzelli, Milan 2001, p. 40.

14. On the relationship between town planning in the capital and Fascism, cf. E. Gentile, *Il fascismo di pietra*, cit.

15. Cf. for this specific case, L. Benevolo, *Roma dal 1870 al 1990*, Laterza, Roma-Bari 1992.

16. G. Melis, *La Macchina imperfetta*, cit., p. 238.

17. Cited in P. di Biagi (ed.), *La grande ricostruzione*, cit., p. 37.

18. "People who have a dwelling but live in overcrowded conditions, with one room for a kitchen, store room and place to eat their meals and a common dormitory and wardrobe, are certainly poor." A. Fanfani, *Colloqui sui poveri, Vita e Pensiero*, Milan 1942, p. 27.

19. P. di Biagi (ed.), *La grande ricostruzione*, cit., p. 18, note.

20. Law no. 43 of February 28, 1949, Provisions for increasing workers' employment, facilitating the construction of houses for workers. In *Gazzetta Ufficiale* no. 54 of 7/3/1949.

21. P. di Biagi (ed.), *La grande ricostruzione*, cit., p. 17.

22. The institute's website storing.ingv.it, collects accounts of all the great earthquakes that have hit in Italy since records began. This is the source for the data presented above. Cf. storing.ingv.it/cfti.

23. Royal Decree Law no.1065 of August 3, 1930, Provisions as a result of the earthquake of July 23, 1930. In *Gazzetta Ufficiale* no. 187 of 11/8/1930, converted by Law no. 1906 of December 29, 1930 n. 1906, in *Gazzetta Ufficiale* no. 39 of 17/2/1931.

24. Cit. in storing.ingv.it/cfti, The Catalogue of Strong Italian Earthquakes describes this earthquake sequence under the following heading, *Terremoto dell'Irpinia e del Vulture 1930*.

25. Ibid.

26. Law no. 1733 of December 28, 1931, Conversion into law of Royal Laws by Decree no. 1841 of June 12, 1931, n. 841, and no. 1003 of July 17, 1931, authorizing further spending for victims of the earthquake of July 23, 1930. In *Gazzetta Ufficiale* no. 22 of 28/1/1932.

27. See storing.ingv.it/cfti.

28. For a short biography of Piero Puricelli, treccani.it/enciclopedia/piero- puricelli_(Dizionario-Biografico). The full

list of his public appointments and parliamentary activity may be found at senato.it, *"senatori dell'Italia fascista."*

29. On seriestoriche.istat.it, transport and road accidents, Table 17.5 – Motor vehicles for which the road tax was paid, by category, Years 1914-2015.

30. Cf. treccani.it/enciclopedia/piero-puricelli_(Dizionario-Biografico).

31. Paul Ginsborg, *A History of Contemporary Italy: Society and Politics 1943-1988*, Penguin Books, London 1990, p. 215.

Chapter 4. Mussolini the Man of Law

1. A. Tasca, *Nascita e avvento del fascismo*, La Nuova Italia, Florence 2002, p. 65 (first edition 1938).

2. E. Gentile, S. M. Di Scala, *Mussolini socialista*, Laterza, Roma-Bari 2015, p. 129.

3. In general, on the figure of Mussolini before the war, cf. E. Gentile, S. M. *Di Scala, Mussolini socialista*, cit., and R. De Felice, *Mussolini il rivoluzionario*, Einaudi, Turin 1995.

4. E. Gentile, *Fascismo*, cit., p. 10.

5. Mussolini's party list in the Milan constituency, one of the few in which he ran and where Fascism had come into being as a movement, obtained 4,657 votes. By way of comparison, the candidate heading the Socialist list, Filippo Turati, obtained 170,201. Cf. *Statistica elezioni generali politiche XXV legislatura*, pp. 76-77. In ISTAT digital library, istat.it

6. R. De Felice, *Mussolini il fascista. La conquista del potere* (1921-1925), Einaudi, Turin 1995, p. 222

7. Silvestri was a somewhat complex figure: as a journalist he was one of Mussolini's accusers at the first Matteotti trial in 1924-25, but testified in his favor at the second trial in 1947. He was dispatched to *confino*, a forced residence in a different part of Italy, in the early 1930s, and drew close to the regime. He was the last journalist to interview Mussolini during the period of the Salò Republic. For a brief account of his life, cf. M. Canali, *Il delitto Matteotti*, il Mulino, Bologna 2015, pp. 269-89.

8. C. Silvestri, *Matteotti, Mussolini e il dramma italiano*, Cavallotti, Milan 1981, p. 58.

9. M. Canali, *Il delitto Matteotti*, cit., p. 40.

10. Cited in R. De Felice, *Mussolini il fascista*, cit. p. 625.

11. M. Canali, *Il delitto Matteotti*, cit., pp. 78-80

12. Ibid., p. 237.

13. R. De Felice, *Mussolini il fascista*, II, cit. p. 625.

14. Ibid., p. 626

15. Speech reproduced in R. De Felice, *Mussolini il fascista*, II, cit. p. 721ff. The importance of this speech in parliament inclines some historians to consider it the moment in which the dictatorship was born in Italy.

16. P. Corner, 'Corruzione di sistema? I "fascisti reali" tra pubblico e privato,' in P. Giovannini e M. Palla (eds), *Il fascismo dalle mani sporche, dittatura, corruzione affarismo*, Laterza, Rome-Bari 2019, p. 10.

17. R. De Felice, *Mussolini il duce. Gli anni del consenso*, Einaudi, Turin 1974, p. 203.

18. P. Corner, 'Corruzione di sistema?', cit., p. 16.

19. M. Franzinelli, *I tentacoli dell'OVRA. Agenti, collaboratori e vittime della polizia politica fascista*, Bollati Boringhieri, Turin 1999, p. 229 ff.

20. A. Petacco, *L'archivio segreto di Mussolini*, Mondadori, Milan 2010, p. III.

21. On this point, cf. M. Franzinelli, *Delatori, spie e confidenti anonimi. L'arma segreta del regime fascista*, Feltrinelli, Milan 2012.

22. R. De Felice, *Mussolini il fascista*, II, cit. pp. 721-22.

23. P. Giovannini, M. Palla (eds), *Il fascismo dalle mani sporche*, cit., p. XV.

24. Dennis Mack Smith dwells on these and other aspects of Mussolini's private life in his book *Mussolini, A Biography*, Knopf, New York 1982.

25. The last days of Mussolini have been the object of vast historiographical, literary and even cinematic investigation. For an overview, in addition to the most comprehensive biographies, cfr. P. Milza, *Gli ultimi giorni di Mussolini*, Longanesi, Milan 2011 and M. Franzinelli, *Il Prigioniero di Salò*, Mondadori, Milano 2012

26. For a reconstruction of resistance to the phenomenon of the mafia since the nineteenth century, U. Santino, *Storia del movimento antimafia*, Editori Riuniti, Romae 2000, and E. Ciconte, *Storia Criminale, la resistibile ascesa di mafia, 'ndrangheta e camorra dall'Ottocento ai giorni nostri*, Rubbettino, Palermo 2008.

27. Royal Decree no. 2047 of December 15, 1921, in approval of the Consoidated Act on the land concession laws. In *Gazzetta Ufficiale* no. 25 of 31/1/1922.

28. Royal Decree Law no. 252 of January 11, 1923, Concerning the abrogation of the rules and regulations on land concession. In *Gazzetta Ufficiale* no. 42 of 20/2/1923, converted by Law no. 473 of April 17, 1925, in *Gazzetta Ufficiale* no. 104 of 5/5/1925.

29. E. J. Hobsbawm, *Primitive Rebels*. Abacus, London 2017, p. 62.

30. S. Lupo, *Storia della mafia. Dalle origini ai nostri giorni*. Donzelli, Milan 2004.

31. E. J. Hobsbawm, *Primitive Rebels*, cit., p. 63-64.

32. E. Ciconte, *Storia Criminale*, cit. p. 276.

33. R. De Felice, *Mussolini il fascista*, cit., p. 28.

34. treccani.it/enciclopedia/cesare-mori_(Dizionario-Biografico).

35. E. Ciconte, *Storia Criminale*, cit., p. 280.

Chapter 5. Mussolini the Economist

1. Treasury Ministry, general public debt management, *Relazione del direttore generale alla commissione parlamentare di vigilanza, Il debito pubblico in Italia 1861-1987* (General Director's report to the parliamentary watch commission. Public debt in Italy 1861-1987), vol. I, Rome 1988, p. 90.

2. Treasury Ministry, cit., p. 33. The debt was finally renegotiated in 1926 with an agreement to repay it in yearly instalments until 1987.

3. Citation taken from R. Petri, *Storia economica d'Italia dalla Grande guerra al miracolo economico (1918-1963)*, il Mulino, Bologna 2002, p. 61.

4. G. Mortara, *Prospettive economiche 1922*, Società Tipografica Leonardo da Vinci, Città di Castello 1922, p. XX, cited in a note by D. Fausto, *Lineamenti dell'evoluzione del debito pubblico in Italia (1861-1961)*, ISTAT, Rome 2005, p. 91.

5. Letter cited in a note by D. Fausto, *Lineamenti* cit., p. 92.

6. G. Matteotti, *Reliquie*, Dall'Oglio, Milan 1965 (first edition, 1924), p. 142.

7. He took out a National Fascist Party membership card in 1921, the year in which the party was founded, when he was writing articles about economics for the *Popolo d'Italia* newspaper. Having been removed from the Finance Ministry, he was one of the party's fiercest critics of the regime's economic policies. Cf. Franco Marcoaldi, 'De Stefani, Alberto,' in *Dizionario biografico degli italiani*, treccani.it.

8. R. Petri, *Storia economica d'Italia*, cit., p. 63.

9. Ibid., p. 65.

10. R. De Felice, *Mussolini il fascista. L'organizzazione dello stato fascista*, Einaudi, Turin 1995, p. 89.

11. For a reconstruction of the methods of application and consequences of the lira-pound sterling exchange rate, cf. M.L. Cavalcanti, *La politica monetaria italiana fra le due guerre (1918-1943)*, Franco Angeli, Milan 2011, pp. 133-42.

12. R. De Felice, *Mussolini il duce*, cit., p. 67.

13. S. La Francesca, *La politica economica del fascismo*, Laterza, Bari, 1973, p. 47.

14. Royal Law by Decree no. 5 of January 23, 1933, Constitution of Institute for Industrial Reconstruction, with offices in Rome. In *Gazzetta Ufficiale* no.19 of 24/1/1933, converted by Law no. 512 of May 3, 1933, in *Gazzetta Ufficiale* no. 128 of 2/6/1933.

15. Royal Decree no. 453 of January 2, 1913, in approval of the annexed Consolidation Act on laws regarding the Administration of the Deposits and Loans Fund, of annexed managements, of the autonomous communal and provincial departments, and of Social Insurance Institutes. In *Gazzetta Ufficiale* no. 170 of 22/7/1913.

16. R. Petri, *Storia economica d'Italia*, cit., p. 98. Petri, in turn, partly cites Fabrizio Barca, *Storia del capitalismo*

italiano dal dopoguerra ad oggi, Donzelli, Roma 1997, p. 9.

17. Royal Decree Law no. 906 of June 24, 1937, Financial provisions relative to the steel industry in which the Institute for Industrial Reconstruction is interested. In *Gazzetta Ufficiale* no. 147 of 26/6/1937, converted by Law no. 2538 of December 30, 1937, in *Gazzetta Ufficiale* no. 44 of 23/2/1938.

18. *Gazzetta Ufficiale* no.147 of 26/6/1937

19. M. Franzinelli, M. Magnani, *Beneduce, il finanziere di Mussolini*, Mondadori, Milan 2009, pp. 229-30.

20. R. Petri, *Storia economica d'Italia*, cit., p. 116.

21. Average annual production in the 1920s, before the "battle" commenced, oscillated between 44 and 60 million quintals. In 1938 production tallied more than 81 million quintals. The figure fell to 70 in subsequent years, after which it was ruined by the war. Cf. seriestoriche.istat.it, Agricoltura, zootecnia e pesca (Agriculture, animal husbandry and fishing), Table 13.9 Production of the principal herbaceous crops: cereals and millable legumes – Years 1861-2015 (in thousands of quintals).

22. All the data presented here are taken, for Italy, from the historical data sets of Finance Ministry and, for other European countries, from the United Nations statistics office, cited in R. De Felice, *Mussolini il duce*, cit., p. 59.

23. R. De Felice, *Mussolini il duce*, cit., p. 59.

24. Ibid., p. 74.

25. Treasury Ministry, public debt general management, cit., p. 39 (note).

26. Ibid., p. 42.

27. F. Guarneri, *Battaglie economiche fra le due guerre*, il Mulino, Bologna 1988, p. 941ff.

28. T. Terhoeven, *Oro alla Patria. Donne, guerra e propaganda nella giornata della fede fascista*, il Mulino, Bologna 2006, p. 190.

29. F. Guarneri, *Battaglie economiche fra le due guerre*, cit., p. 941 e ssg.

30. H. Gibson (ed.), *The Ciano Diaries, 1939-1943: The Complete and Unabridged Diaries of Count Galeazzo Ciano, Italian Minister for Foreign Affairs, 1936-1943,* Simon Publications, New York 1945, p. 207.

31. M. Sorrentino, G. Vecchi, 'Le condizioni di vita degli italiani: nutrizione,' in, G. Vecchi, *In ricchezza e in povertà. Il benessere degli italiani dall'Unità a oggi,* il Mulino, Bologna 2011, p. 32.

Chapter 6. Mussolini the Feminist

1. G. Galeotti, *Storia del voto alle donne in Italia. Alle radici del difficile rapporto tra donne e politica,* Biblink, Rome 2006, p. 76.

2. G. Galeotti, *Storia del voto alle donne in Italia,* cit., p. 30. The author takes the citation from a speech in B. Mussolini, *Opera Omnia* (E. and D. Susmel eds), Florence 1951-1980, vol. XIX, p. 215.

3. Law no. 2125 of November 22, 1925, Admission of women to the local electorate. In *Gazzetta Ufficiale* no. 285 of 9/12/1925

4. Law no. 237 of February 4, 1926, Institution of the Podestà and the Municipal Council in Communes with a population of no more than 5,000 inhabitants. In *Gazzetta Ufficiale* no. 40 of 18/2/1926.

5. Lieutenant Decree Law no. 23 of February 1945, Extension of the right to vote to women. In *Gazzetta Ufficiale* n.22 of 20/2/1945.

6. Lieutenant Decree Law n. 74 of March 10, 1946, Rules and regulations for the election of deputies to the Constituent Assembly. In *Gazzetta Ufficiale* no. 60 of 12/3/1946 – Ordinary Suppement no. 60.

7. Law no. 2277 of December 10, 1925, Protection of and assistance to mothers and children. In *Gazzetta Ufficiale* no. 4 of 7/1/1926.

8. *Gazzetta Ufficiale* no. 4 of 7/1/1926.

9. Royal Decree Law no. 654 of March 22, 1934, Protection of the maternity of female workers. In *Gazzetta Ufficiale* no. 99 of 27/4/1934, converted by Law no. 1347 of July 5, 1934, in *Gazzetta Ufficiale* no. 199 of 25/8/1934.

10. G. Galeotti, *Storia del voto alle donne in Italia. Alle rad- ici del difficile rap- porto tra donne e politica*, cit. Biblink, Rome 2006, p. 92.

11.Royal Decree no. 1084 of June 6, 1925, Regulation for the private and legally recognised institutes of secondary education and for the creation, assignment of royal status and transformation of schools. In *Gazzetta Ufficiale* no. 154 of 6/7/1925

12. Royal Decree no. 1084 of June 6, 1925, art. 50.

13. Royal Decree no. 2480 of December 9, 1926, Regulation for competitions for reaching posts in Royal secondary schools and for qualifications for teaching professionally in secondary schools. In *Gazzetta Ufficiale* no. 73 of 29/3/1927, Art. 11, "Men and women are admitted indistinctly to competitions and qualification examinations, with the exception of classes IV, V (limited to competitions for technical high schools), VI and VII (limited to competitions for secondary schools with the emphasis on humanities or sciences), according to the table annexed, which are reserved to men, and competitions and qualification examinations for posts as gardening mistresses in teacher training schools."

14. Royal Decree Law no. 1554 of November 28, 1933, n. 1554, Rules and regulations on the recruitment of women in the State Administration. In *Gazzetta Ufficiale* no. 277 of 30/11/1933, converted by Law no. 221 of January 18 1934, in *Gazzetta Ufficiale* no. 48 of 27/2/1934.

15. Royal Decree no. 383 of March 3, 1934, Approval of the Consolidated Act on communal and provincial law. In *Gazzetta Ufficiale* no. 65 of 17/3/1934. Ordinary Supplement no. 65. Article 68 in particular envisages that only women possessing given requisites such as the mothers of war victims, medalled women etc. could sit on *Consulte*, the bodies that replaced elective communal councils in the Fascist period.

16. Royal Decree Law no. 1514 of September 5, 1938, Rules and regulations governing the recruitment of female personnel in public and private posts. In *Gazzetta Ufficiale*

no. 228 of 5/10/1938 G.U. n.228 converted by Law no. 77 of January 5, 1939, in *Gazzetta Ufficiale* no. 30 of 6/2/1939. Art. 1 "Recruitment of women in posts in the state administration and other public bodies or institutions, to which they are admitted on the basis of provisions in force, as well as in private posts, is limited to a maximum proportion of 10 per cent of the number of said posts. Public administrations shall reserve the right to establish a lower percentage for appointments and posts. Public administrations and private companies with fewer than ten employees shall not recruit any woman as an employee. Exception shall be made for private companies in the case of female relatives or relatives by marriage to the fifth degree of the company's owner."

17. Art. 587 of the Penal Code approved by Royal Decree no. 1398 of October 19, 1930. Article abrogated by art. 1 of Law no. 442 of August 5, 1981, Abrogation of the criminal relevance of honor killing.

18. Law no. 442 of August 5, 1981.

19. After the death of the Duce, Rachele Guidi even wrote books in which, despite everything, she supported and defended her husband's reputation. The first was published in 1948 with the familiar title of *La mia vita con Benito* (Arnoldo Mondadori, Milan 1948).

Chapter 7. Mussolini the Condottiere and Statesman

1. R. De Felice, *Mussolini il rivoluzionario* (1883-1920), Einaudi, Turin 2018, p. 46. More generally, on Mussolini's experience in Switzerland, S. Visconti, 'L'educazione rivoluzionaria di un romagnolo in Svizzera,' in E. Gentile, S.M. Di Scala, *Mussolini socialista*, Laterza, Roma-Bari 2015, pp. 3-36.

2. E. Gentile, *Fascismo*, cit., p. 8.

3. A. Del Boca, *Italiani, Brava gente? Un mito duro a morire*, Neri Pozza, Vicenza 2005, p. 44.

4. For a potted biography of the *gerarca*, who was at Mussolini's side from the March on Rome to the vote against him on July 25, 1943, see treccani.it/ enciclopedia/ de-vecchi-cesare-maria_(Dizionario-Biografico).

5. G. Rochat, *Le guerre italiane (1935-1943). Dall'Impero d'Etiopia alla disfatta*, Einaudi, Turin 2008, p. 23.

6. Ibid., p. 37.

7. Staggering quantities were taken to the theater of war: more specifically, 60,000 artillery projectiles filled with arsine and about 3,300 aerial bombs containing 220 kilos of mustard gas each (cf. Rochat, *Le guerre italiane*, cit. pp. 66-67).

8. Angelo del Boca cites a number of accounts in which Vittorio Mussolini himself describes the air battle against the Ethiopians as more a hunting party than a fight: "An Abyssinian with a rifle was running southwards, a nice burst of machine gun fire and the Abyssinian hit the floor. It was an isolated manhunt as usual and every plane did its own thing, searching every hollow to sniff out Abyssinians." Cf. V. Mussolini, *In volo sulle Ambe*, Sansoni, Florence 1937, p. 52, cited in A. Del Boca, *Italiani, Brava gente?*, cit., pp. 189-90.

9. The Africanist historian Richard Pankhurst cast light on the bombing, which the regime first denied, then claimed to be accidental, in 1997 with his study 'Il bombardamento fascista sulla Croce Rossa durante l'invasione dell'Etiopia (1935-1936)', in *Studi Piacentini*, no. 21, 1997, pp. 129-54

10. G. Rochat, *Le guerre italiane*, cit., p. 88

11. A. Del Boca, *Italiani, Brava gente?*, cit., p. 167.

12. Out of 50,000 men sent to Spain, Rochat counts 29,302 members of the Fascist militia and, with due distinctions, a large number of volunteers. Alongside them were as many as 20,000 effectives (cf. G. Rochat, *Le guerre italiane*, cit., p. 105).

13. A. Del Boca, *Italiani, Brava gente?*, cit., p. 45. Under the Royal Decree of June 20, 1935, No. 1010, Mussolini decided that Italians had to devote their Saturday afternoons to sports and cultural activities in a paramilitary manner. In Italian, *il sabato fascista*. (translator's note).

14. G. Rochat, *Le guerre italiane*, cit., p.113.

15. One of the most famous cases was that of General Cavallero, who for many years held posts both in the army and in conglomerates in the armaments industry (he was president of Ansaldo). For a summary of his disastrous and dishonest trajectory as an armaments supervisor, see

P. Ferrari, 'Cavallero tra industria e Stato maggiore,' in P. Giovannini and M. Palla (eds), *Il fascismo dalle mani sporche*, cit., pp. 86-106.

16. "The War in Spain had not taken Italy to the center of international politics as the *Duce* had hoped; the alliance with Germany, opposed by a section of the party, by the king and by the population, wasn't producing the results hoped for and the Germans always moved on the international scene without coordination with Mussolini. The declaration of war against Poland was one of the many episodes in which Hitler told Italy after the deed was done." H. Gibson (ed.), *The Ciano Diaries, 1939-1943: The Complete and Unabridged Diaries of Count Galeazzo Ciano, Italian Minister for Foreign Affairs, 1936-1943*, Simon Publications, New York 1945.

17. G. Rochat, *Le guerre italiane*, cit., p. 250

18. Hitler himself sought to refuse the Italian soldiers: "Decisive help, *Duce*, you can always provide by reinforcing your troops in North Africa," was the answer he had relayed after yet another offer of soldiers against the USSR (cf. G. Rochat, *Le guerre italiane*, cit., p. 378).

19. G. Rochat, *Le guerre italiane*, cit., pp. 383-87.

Chapter 8. Mussolini the Humanitarian

1. The claim is made by Silvio Berlusconi in the famous interview he gave to the British magazine *The Spectator* in September 2003. On that occasion the former Italian premier compared the *Duce* to Saddam Hussein, saying, "That was a much more benign dictatorship ... Mussolini never murdered anyone, Mussolini sent people on holiday to confine them." *The Spectator*, September 6, 2003.

2. Sentence of the Court of Cassation no. 8108/2018. "Fascist Salute: Court of Cassation: 'Not a crime if commemorative.'", *La Repubblica*, February 20, 2018.

3. Royal Decree no. 51 of February 9, 1902, n. 51, On the legal system in the Eritrea Colony, in *Gazzetta Ufficiale*, no. 74 of 29/3/1902.

4. The poem "The White Man's Burden", written in 1899, speaks of the difficult and thankless task of the white man,

who has to deliver civilization around the world. Cf. R. J. Kipling, *Collected Poems*, Wordsworth Editions, London 1994

5. L. Martone, *Giustizia coloniale. Modelli e prassi penali per i sudditi d'Africa dall'età giolittiana al fascismo*, Jovene Editore, Naples 2002, p. 30.

6. Speech reported in *Il Popolo d'Italia*, no. 142, May 24, 1918.

7. E. Gentile, *Fascismo di pietra*, cit., p. 47

8. Parliamentary proceedings, Chamber of Deputies, 16th Legislature, first session, debates, round of June 21, 1921, p. 89. In storia.camera.it.

9. E. Gentile, *Fascismo*, cit., p. 6.

10. E. Gentile, *Fascismo*, cit., p. 247.

11. For the violence that took Mussolini to power in the period, cf. G. Salvemini, *The Origins of Fascism in Italy*, Harper & Row, New York 1973.

12. G. Salvemini, *The Origins of Fascism in Italy*, cit.

13. E. Gentile, *Fascismo*, cit., p. 235.

14. A. Del Boca, *Italiani, Brava gente?*, cit., p. 167

15. A. Del Boca, *Italiani, Brava gente?*, cit., p. 178.

16. Ibid., p. 180.

17. G. Rochat, *Le guerre italiane*, cit., p. 13

18. For an overview of the politics of options in Alto Adige, cf. F. Scarano, *Tra Mussolini e Hitler. Le opzioni dei sudtirolesi nella politica estera fascista*, Franco Angeli, Milan 2012. On Fascist violence in the Balkans, in addition to Del Boca, already cited, cf. G. Oliva, *Si ammazza troppo poco. I crimini di guerra italiani, 1940-1943*, Mondadori, Milan 2007.

19. C. Di Sante, *Italiani senza onore. I crimini in Jugoslavia e i processi negati, 1941-1951*, Ombre Corte, Verona 2005, p. 39.

20. F. Focardi, *Il cattivo tedesco e il bravo italiano. La rimozione delle colpe della seconda guerra mondiale*, Laterza, Rome-Bari 2013, p. 132.

21. Cf. D. Rodogno, *Il nuovo ordine mediterraneo. Le politiche di occupazione dell'Italia fascista in Europa* (1940-1943), Bollati Boringhieri, Turin 2003, p. 88. The historian uses this definition to frame Italy's essentially racist and

imperialist approach to the government of its occupied territories.

22. Law no. 999 of July 6, 1933, Organic Legal System for Eritrea and Somalia. In *Gazzetta Ufficiale*, no. 189 of 16/8/1933.

23. N. Labanca, *Oltremare. Storia dell'espansione coloniale italiana*, il Mulino, Bologna 2007, p. 355.

24. G. Stefani, *Colonia per maschi. Italiani in Africa orientale: una storia di genere*, Ombre Corte, Verona 2007, p. 136.

25. On July 14, 1938, a group of Fascist scientists published an article entitled 'Fascism and the Problems of Race' in *Il Giornale d'Italia*. It was then reprinted in the first number of the review *La difesa della razza* on August 5, 1938. The full text of the article is published on the ANPI (Italian National Association of Partisans) website at anpi. it/storia/114/il-manifesto-della-razza-1938. However, according to the account of Galeazzo Ciano, the *Duce*'s son-in-law, the framework of the document was not the spontaneous work of the Italian academics: "On July 14 [...] the *Duce* informs me of the publication by *Il Giornale d'Italia* of an article on racial questions. It's presented as being written by a group of scholars under the aegis of the Ministry of Popular Culture. He tells me that actually he wrote it nearly all by himself." In H. Gibson (ed.), *The Ciano Diaries, 1939-1943*.

26. Order paper of the Fascist National Party, October 26, 1938.

27. Decree-law no. 1728 of November 17, 1938, Provisions for the defense of the Italian race. In *Gazzetta Ufficiale* no. 264 of 19/11/1938, converted by Law no. 274 January 5, 1939. In *Gazzetta Ufficiale* no. 48 of 27/2/1939.

28. G. Mosse, The Crisis of German Ideology, H. Fertig, New York 1998.

29. F. Focardi, *Il cattivo tedesco e il bravo italiano*, cit., p. 117.

30. Ibid., p. 113.

31. Ibid., pp. 116-17.

32. D. Bidussa, *Il mito del bravo italiano*, il Saggiatore, Milan 1994, p. 79

33. In H. Gibson (ed.), *The Ciano Diaries, 1939-1943*, cit., p. 202.

34. In H. Gibson (ed.), *The Ciano Diaries, 1939-1943*, cit., pp. 326-327.

35. R. De Felice, *Mussolini il duce*, cit., p. 339

36. G. Melis, *La macchina imperfetta*, cit., p. 168.

37. Law no. 660 of April 3, 1926, Extension of the powers of Prefects. In *Gazzetta Ufficiale*, no. 97 of 27/4/1926

38. F. Focardi, *Il cattivo tedesco e il bravo ita*liano, cit., p.149.

Assorted Information

1. Law no, 2307 of December 31, 1925, Provisions on the periodical press. In *Gazzetta Ufficiale* no. 3 of 5/1/1926.

2. Royal Decree no. 773 of June 18, 1931, Approval of the Consolidated Act on public safety laws. In *Gazzetta Ufficiale* no. 146 of 26/6/1931 – Ordinary Supplement no. 146.

3. Art. 112: "It is forbidden to produce, introduce onto state territory, acquire, possess, export, for commercial or distributive purposes, or spread written material, drawings, images or other objects of any kind contrary to the political, social or economic systems constituted in the state or harmful to state prestige or its authority or offensive to national sentiment and common and public decency. In *Gazzetta Ufficiale* no. 146 of 26/6/1931 – Ordinary Supplement no. 146.

4. Royal Decree no, 1175 of September 14, 1931. Consolidated Act on local finance. In *Gazzetta Ufficiale* no. 214 of 16/9/1931 – Ordinary Supplement no. 214.

5. Royal Decree no, 1175 of September 14, 1931. Consolidated Act in local finance. In *Gazzetta Ufficiale* no. 214 of 16/9/1931 – Ordinary Supplement no. 214.

6. Data collected in *Popolazione e società, struttura ed evoluzione della popolazione ai censimenti*, seriestoriche.istat.it.

7. Ibid.

8. A.Treves, *Le nascite e la politica nell'Italia del Novecento*, Led, Milan 2001, pp. 119-25.

9. *Popolazione e società, struttura ed evoluzione della popolazione ai censimenti*, seriestoriche.istat.it.

10. treccani.it/enciclopedia/il-fascismo-e-la-scienza.

ALSO FROM BARAKA BOOKS

NONFICTION

Patriots, Traitors and Empires, The Story of Korea's Struggle for Freedom
Stephen Gowans

Bigotry on Broadway, An Anthology Edited by
Ishmael Reed and Carla Blank

*A Distinct Alien Race, The Untold Story
of Franco-Americans*
David Vermette

The Einstein File, The FBI's Secret War on the World's Most Famous Scientist
Fred Jerome

Montreal and the Bomb
Gilles Sabourin

The Question of Separatism, Quebec and the Struggle Over Sovereignty
Jane Jacobs

Stolen Motherhood, Surrogacy and Made-to-Order Children
Maria De Koninck

Still Crying for Help, The Failure of Our Mental Healthcare Services
Sadia Messaili

FICTION

Maker, A Novel
Jim Upton

Exile Blues
Douglas Gary Freeman

Things Worth Burying
Matt Mayr

Fog
Rana Bose

Yasmeen Haddad Loves Joanasi Maqaittik
Carolyn Marie Souaid

MIX
Paper from
responsible sources
FSC® C100212
FSC
www.fsc.org

Printed by Imprimerie Gauvin
Gatineau, Québec